Health, Wealth and Happiness
—a key to successful living—

Foreword

S0-BSI-606

Millions of people are searching for the formula for success, health, wealth, and happiness. Benjamin Franklin has become a symbol of wisdom because of the proverbs he wrote. But the greatest treasure-house of wisdom—Proverbs—has been overlooked. It was written by the wisest of men, Solomon.

Few books have ever been written on Proverbs. Therefore it required four and one-half months to prepare the outline of this book, so the many proverbs could be catalogued under fifty-two chapter themes. We have endeavored to deal with every verse in Proverbs, applying it to its theme.

Proverbs reveals the secrets of successful living. It is practical and applicable to our day, for truth never changes. It was written particularly for youth, but adults will find it applicable to life of all ages.

We have written on Proverbs, hoping that it would be useful as a book for daily devotions. But we also had in mind the possibility that it would prove useful as a text for fifty-two lessons to be used in Sunday School, or else in a weekly Bible study. Its contents should encompass the entire Bible as it is studied.

The treasures of Proverbs are rare gems of beauty and value. We pray you will profit by reading this book.

Many a pitfall in life will be avoided by those who will apply the great truths of Proverbs to their everyday life.

Ralph W. Neighbour, Sr.

Health, Wealth and Happiness
—a key to successful living—

Ralph W. Neighbour, Sr., D.D.

G. Allen Fleece Library
Columbia International University
Columbia, SC 29203

timothy books
Newtown Industrial Commons
Newtown, PA 18940

G. Allen Fleece Library
Columbia International University
Columbia, SC 29203

Health, Wealth and Happiness
Ralph W. Neighbour, Sr., D.D.

ISBN: 0-914964-01-1

© 1974
Timothy Books division of
Hearthstone Publications, Inc.

PRINTED IN U.S. OF AMERICA

Contents

Be Wise 7
The Wise Man 10
Shun Evil 13
Christ Rejectors 16
The Quest for Knowledge 19
Three Things to Remember 23
Three Worthwhile Admonitions 27
Blessings in Chastisement 31
Life's Greatest Discovery 34
Let Us Do Good 37
The Path of the Just 40
Warning Against Sexual Sin 43
Sound Business Principles 46
Shun Adultery 49
Christ, the Great Deliverer 52
Life's Greatest Choice 56
Three Rewards for Righteousness 59
Three Divine Blessings 63
Three Kindred Evils 66
The Blessedness of Giving 69
Winning Souls 73
The Poor Rich Man 76
The Folly of Procrastination 79
The Value of Discipline 83
Fools Mock Sin 86
Man's Ways Are Not God's Ways 89
The Backslider 92
A True Witness 95
The Fear of the Lord 98
Righteousness Exalteth a Nation 101
Thy God Seeth Thee 104
Peacemakers 107
A Comparison of Values 110
God Hears Prayer 113
God Is Sovereign 116

Self Mastery   120
The Hour of Temptation   124
Avoid Alcoholic Beverages   128
Man's Dependence Upon God   132
Oppress Not the Poor   135
Shun Falsehood and Dishonesty   139
Don't Be a Glutton   142
Give Your Heart to God   145
The Parable of the Neglected Field   148
Family Relationship   151
For Peace of Mind   154
New Testament Truths Based on Proverbs   157
Eight Well Known Adages   160
Warning to Sinners   163
Who Is God's Son?   166
Lessons from Nature   169
The Perfect Wife   172

Be Wise

"The proverbs of Solomon the son of David, king of Israel" (Proverbs 1:1).

A truly wise person will gain wisdom from the wise. No one man can experiment and gain knowledge of all of the vast areas of human and divine wisdom; life would be too brief for this to be possible, and no single individual has the capacity to excel in all areas of knowledge.

Solomon, the wisest of men, was endowed with wisdom by God. When he became ruler of Israel, recognizing his human limitations, he sought wisdom from God that he might be a worthy ruler. God heard his prayer and made him the wisest of all men (II Chronicles 1:10–12).

Fortunately, Solomon was a prolific writer, sharing his God-given wisdom with the world. He wrote three thousand proverbs and one thousand and five songs (I Kings 4:32). He clearly stated the purpose of his writings: They are goads to prod us into action, and nails to control our actions (Ecclesiastes 12:9–12).

It is obvious that the complete Book of Proverbs was not written at one time. The first nine chapters are a preface of connected poetic addresses. Chapters 10–24 make up the first volume of actual proverbs which are short, terse, detached sayings, each complete in itself (Proverbs 10:1). Chapter 25–29 constitute the second volume. Additional proverbs of Solomon, which had not originally been included in the book, were added by the scribes of Hezekiah (Proverbs 25:1). The author of Chapter 30 is named as Agur (Proverbs 30:1). However, it is the opinion of some that Agur is but another name of Solomon. Other scholars are of the opinion that Agur was an Arabian king. Proverbs 31:1 credits King Lemuel as the author of this final chapter. It is possible that the name Lemuel is the pet name that King Solomon's own mother gave him, but there is always the

7

possibility that King Lemuel was another king other than Solomon.

THE PURPOSE OF PROVERBS

The key verse of Proverbs is 1:7—"The fear of the Lord is the beginning of knowledge." Proverbs is a book of Christian ethics, telling us how to live, revealing the secrets of successful living. It teaches us everyday common sense. Surely we should spend much time in this book, for it is a treasure house of practical principles which are essential guidelines for successful business and a worthwhile life.

Proverbs proves that successful living begins with faith and a knowledge of God and spiritual things. In other words, it pays to be a Christian.

Proverbs is particularly slanted toward the teen-ager (Proverbs 1:18; 2:1; 4:1). Soon half of our entire population will be youth. Youth will shape the world in which we live. Furthermore, the urge of sin is greatest during the teen years. Life's choices are made during this period of life. The future of the home, of Christianity, and of the entire nation is in the lap of our youth. And Proverbs is their book!

At the same time, the wisdom of this book is also adaptable to mature adults. Proverbs 8:1–5 says that wisdom cries out to all men. To ignore the voice of this book is to be a fool. How sad it is that so few ever read Proverbs, and fewer still ever study it and obey it. Some of the richest treasures of precious promises are to be found in Proverbs. One may live by these treasures.

A young man graduating from a high school in Pennsylvania was congratulated by the professor of science. "What do you plan to do with your education," the professor asked.

"I intend to be a tramp," the honor student replied.

"Why," the professor asked.

"Because the world offers me nothing to live for," the graduate answered.

Proverbs offers youth something to live for—Christ. As Paul said, "For to me to live is Christ" (Philippians 1:21). Life without objective and purpose becomes dull, but a sin-sick world only becomes a challenge for the person who knows the Lord Jesus Christ, who is called "Wisdom" in Proverbs. Proverbs is the answer to disillusioned youth in a day of decay.

BE WISE AND HEAR

"A wise man will hear, and will increase learning; and a man of understanding shall attain unto wise counsels: to understand a proverb, and the interpretation; the words of the wise, and their dark sayings" (Proverbs 1:5, 6).

The original Hebrew of the word proverb is *mashal.* It means *to be like,* or *to represent.* A proverb then is a precept. It is a sermon in a nutshell. It is the law which governs life. It is a parable which requires much thought to crack the shell before one can enjoy the meat of its meaning. A proverb is reasonable and challenges thought.

When the prodigal son went into a far country, he was not thinking. He was blindly following his lusts and emotional desires. He did not stop to consider the consequences or ultimate end of his journey. Had he read and studied the Book of Proverbs, he might not have started out on his aimless journey. Proverbs challenges us to determine the course of life and not to follow ambitions blindly. One should read this book daily and study its precepts. It pays to profit by the experience of another, particularly if that person is the wisest of men who has been inspired by the Holy Spirit.

If someone were to offer you the secret for making great wealth so that you could become a millionaire, would you ignore that person? Proverbs does just that! Much more, it offers secrets of successful living! Obey these secrets.

The Wise Man

The fear of the Lord is the beginning of knowledge: but fools despise wisdom and instruction (Proverbs 1:7).

KNOWLEDGE BEGINS WITH GOD

Atheists call themselves *free-thinkers* and imply that atheism will liberate the mind and make one free. But the very opposite is true. Unbelief blinds the mind and the heart, producing foolish superstitions. Atheism ignores the facts and basic principles of life. Jesus said, "Ye shall know the truth, and the truth shall make you free" (John 8:32).

Knowledge has its beginning with God. Not until a person seeks and receives Christ as Saviour does he begin to progress intellectually. The new birth frees the mind from all of the superstitions of paganism and unbelief. Foolish ritualism and human bigotries are broken and cast aside. The mind is at last free to be enlightened with the divine revelation of Scripture and true science.

Many of the world's great men have proudly witnessed to the fact they were Christians. They have attributed their success to the strength and courage that their faith gave them.

Civilization is the flower that blooms in the friendly environment of Christianity. Social advancement flourishes in the soil of faith in God. Wherever missionaries have planted the banner of the cross, civilization has followed.

On the other hand, evil rulers and men of violence, who have caused immeasurable sorrow and trouble for the human race, have lacked faith and belief in God. Not one evil ruler has been a Christian. Not one wicked man or criminal has been a child of God. Does this not speak for itself? Should we not acknowledge the truth of our text? "Knowledge begins with the fear of the Lord." Shouldn't we seek the Lord early in life?

Atheism boasts of its intellectualism, but what college or institution of learning has atheism ever produced? What hospital or place of mercy has it ever given birth to? Christianity, however, has built schools, hospitals, mission stations, and centers of learning. Atheism captures and steals them. Christianity has blazed the trails of civilization, penetrating cannibal tribes and changing savages into intellectual, social beings. Civilization is the fruit that grows on the tree of Christianity.

The knowledge of the Lord does not lead to riots, civil wars, or crime. Violence is the fruit of godlessness. The answer to crime is Christ.

Godless philosophies, such as the teachings of Kant, Karl Marx, Neitzsche, and Darwin, have left the world in a shambles. The idea of the superman emanates from Neitzsche and is based on the evolution theory. These false philosophies have produced two world wars and world communism. Again we say, "The fear of the Lord is the beginning of wisdom."

Jesus Christ said, "The truth shall make you free." Those who fear the Lord learn to become masters of themselves. No longer do they need to be slaves to sin and lust. They are free men! The folly of evolution, idolatry, slavery, and human intolerance are no longer masters of the man who has made Christ both Saviour and Lord.

Womanhood is enslaved where Christ is not known and where unbelief reigns. Christianity liberates the woman and gives her a rightful place in society. Human slavery of all kinds, including mental and moral slavery, is broken when men seek and know the Lord. "The fear of the Lord is the beginning of wisdom."

THE VALUE OF PARENTAL INSTRUCTION

My son, hear the instruction of thy father, and forsake not the law of thy mother (Proverbs 1:8).

God knew that children would need the guidance and help of adults to save them from tragic mistakes in life. It is God's plan that parents direct their children in the way of truth.

A newborn babe would soon die without parental supervision and care. And as that child grows he would fall into many pitfalls of danger and sin without guidance.

Each generation learns from the preceding generation and profits thereby. How foolish and ignorant it would be to ignore past knowledge and to repeat the mistakes and failures of those who have lived before us. Each generation should add to the knowledge of the previous generation and not waste time struggling through the same bogs of error that former generations did. To ignore parental instruction is inexcusable ignorance!

To give spiritual guidance, a parent must know and worship the Lord. A child needs to prepare to face life with all of its vicissitudes and dangers. And if he is wise he will learn from his parents and not ignore his father's law or his mother's teachings.

Laws are given as guidelines so that we will know the right path to walk. To ignore such laws is to invite disaster. Those who rebel against them ignore experience and knowledge. A rebel, then, is a fool!

THE VALUE OF CHRISTIAN CHARACTER

The virtues which accure from Christian faith adorn the *For they shall be an ornament of grace unto thy head, and chains about thy neck* (Proverbs 1:9).

character of those who believe in God. True beauty is not physical but spiritual. Spiritual virtues adorn us more than jewelry and these virtues are kindness, goodness, love, graciousness, courage, thankfulness, and self-control.

Christian virtue is practical. God's laws prepare us and train us to be honorable in business, to be wise in every choice we make in life, to be careful in the selection of friends and companions. We should wear Christian virtues about our neck as we would a necklace; they will bring honor and glory.

Shun Evil

My son, if sinners entice thee, consent thou not. (Proverbs 1:10). *Cast in thy lot among us; let us all have one purse* (Proverbs 1:14). *For their feet run to evil, and make haste to shed blood* (Proverbs 1:16).

An important part of the Christian life is our choice of companions. It is utterly impossible to walk in the Christian path and to make a bosom companion of a sinner at the same time. We must choose between Christ and the Christ rejector, though he may be our dearest friend. We cannot walk in God's way and be a friend to the world at the same time; the pathways go in opposite directions. Long before we choose what we will or will not do, we must choose our companions. Evil companions will not wish to be our friends unless we live as they live.

Some years ago, a young woman openly accepted Christ. She vowed she would no longer live in sin. The following night her fiancé, a godless individual, called to see her.

"Let's go to the tavern and have a drink," he suggested.

"Oh, no!" she remonstrated.

He suggested one thing after another, and each suggestion was rejected and refused. Finally, in anger he said, "What's the matter with you? You sound as if you have religion!"

"No, not religion," she said, "but I do have Christ in my heart. I accepted Him as my Saviour last night, and I'm not interested in doing the things I used to do."

He was stunned. After a moment of consideration, he asked, "Is there anything we can do together? Now don't ask me to go to church with you, for I won't go."

She hesitated. She had not considered that her decision to accept Christ as Saviour would so completely change her life and desires. Finally, she answered him, "No, come to think of it, there isn't anything that we can really enjoy together.

My entire interests in life have changed. We are journeying in opposite directions. We no longer have anything in common. If I am to go the way of Christ, then our paths must part forever."

She paused, silently took the engagement ring from her finger and returned it to him.

If you choose evil companions, they will endeavor to entice you to do evil; either you will yield or else you will be compelled to part company with them.

We live in a day of organized crime; gangsterism has grown into national proportions, threatening the very existence of law and order. Always Christians have been compelled to choose between evil and good, but today we must choose between organized crime and Christ. We must carefully choose companions and associations as never before. You cannot choose the right way and the wrong crowd; they are incompatible. Before you make your choice, carefully consider the consequences for your choice will lead to heaven or hell. Your choice will be an everlasting choice.

If you choose the wrong company, you will share in their crimes and guilt. A fourteen-year-old lad in Michigan picked up an unknown companion while drinking a soda in the drug store. That night his newly found companion suggested playing a game: holding up a filling station. "It's not for real," he said. "We'll just play a joke."

But the unknown companion did actually hold up the man at the filling station, robbed him, and fled. Both boys were caught and sent to prison, the innocent with the guilty.

A prisoner at a Federal Penitentiary told how he took a job driving a truck. He did not know he was part of a gang, running a liquor truck in defiance of the law. When he discovered he was part of a gang, he tried to quit his job, but he was threatened with death if he quit. Soon after, he was arrested, tried and sentenced to prison for many years.

Two brothers wishing to make a quick dollar to pay the doctor's bills for their ailing father, hired a hoodlum to assist them in a holdup of a bank. The hoodlum shot and killed the teller of the bank. Both brothers were apprehended with the hoodlum, and died in the electric chair with him. They had no intention to commit murder.

The most important companion you will ever choose will be your marriage mate. A wrong choice for marriage

may completely ruin your life and bring you to complete
ruin.

REFUSE EVIL DESIGNS

*If they say, Come with us, let us lay wait for blood,
let us lurk privily for the innocent without cause: let
us swallow them up alive as the grave; and whole, as
those that go down into the pit* (Proverbs 1:11–12).

Often evil is designed as an act of persecution against
those who are righteous. Nothing is more cowardly, unfair,
and unsportsmanlike than crime. Criminals never attack
their victim on an equal basis; they always outnumber their
victim. Criminals are cowardly.

The criminal never considers how precious his own life is
to him. He refuses to grant to others his own desire to live.
He never considers the heartache, sorrow, suffering, and
trouble he causes. A thief is a cheat. His motive is greed, and
his ambitions are selfish. His life is contrary to the teachings of Christ. The more criminals there are, the more sorrow there will be.

The criminal's gain is almost worthless. He dare not use it
openly or he will be detected. Other criminals steal from him,
blackmailing him as a price for secrecy. Crime is costly, and
its gains are valueless.

THE FOLLY OF CRIME

*Surely in vain the net is spread in the sight of any
bird. And they lay wait for their own blood; they lurk
privily for their own lives. So are the ways of every
one that is greedy of gain; which taketh away the life
of the owners thereof* (Proverbs 1:17–19).

Crime never pays. There is no perfect crime. Sooner or
later, the criminal will be apprehended and he will spend
precious years of his life in prison. Modern crime detection
methods are so perfect a criminal will find it almost impossible to escape the law.

In the end the criminal will go to an early grave. His
death is likely to be violent. His life will be filled with
bitterness and emptiness. Such a life is unrewarding.

The plunder he will accumulate will gnaw at his soul.

Christt Rejectors

Wisdom crieth without; she uttereth her voice in the streets: she crieth in the chief place of concourse, in the openings of the gates: in the city she uttereth her words, saying, How long, ye simple ones, will ye love simplicity? and the scorners delight in their scorning, and fools hate knowledge? Turn you at my reproof: behold, I will pour out my spirit unto you, I will make known my words to you (Proverbs 1:20–23).

The word *Wisdom* is personified in verse 20 indicating that the name refers to God, or God in the person of Christ. Later in our study of Proverbs we will have a complete study on this subject. The Person who is calling us to God and salvation is none other than God himself. It is only sensible to be a Christian; it is folly to reject Christ and to live without God and without hope of heaven.

As our Scripture indicates, God speaks to us in many places, and in many ways. His voice never ceases to warn us and to beckon us to come to God for salvation.

We hear the voice of God on the streets. Every time there is an accident He warns us to prepare our own souls for the time of trouble, or even death. On the streets we see the mass of humanity pass by. We see the tragic implications of sin. The broken bodies of sin-ridden derelicts warn us again and again to live a righteous life.

We are constantly reminded of the brevity of life as we see old age creeping upon us. This changing world speaks to us, reminding us that it does not pay to live only for the things of this world. This materialistic world is a dying world. God calls to us and urges us to live for and prepare for another world which is eternal in the heavens.

The headlines of the newspaper cry out the history of mankind as things transpire. We see the hopelessness of man-

16

kind without God and Christ. These changing times remind us that there is no solid footing until we take our stand upon the Rock of Ages.

God inquires in verse 22 how long it will take for us to awaken to the dangers of life without God. Only the simple minded ignore the need of their soul's salvation. Some people are very slow to heed the warnings of God. God is patient, but He will not always chide. (See Psalm 103:8, 9). His mercy may endure forever, but there is an end of opportunity to turn to God. Sudden death may remove us from the land of opportunity. God's Word warns, "Boast not thyself of tomorrow" (Proverbs 27:1).

A woman in New York was convicted of sin and her need of Christ. Instead of yielding, however, she forced her children to leave a worship service during an invitation. That Saturday she fell and broke her arm. She knew God was speaking to her but she refused to yield. The following week her baby died. Then she turned to Christ. "Why was I so stubborn?" she asked. "Why didn't I come to God before tragedy struck and awakened me to my need?"

God offers (verse 23) to help those who seek salvation. He offers His Holy Spirit, who will bring conviction, light, guidance, and life itself, to those who seek the Lord. In addition to the Holy Spirit, He offers His Word as a final authority for salvation and assurance of life eternal. "God says it; I believe it; that settles it!" (See I John 5:13).

THE FOLLY OF REJECTING CHRIST

Because I have called, and ye refused; I have stretched out my hand, and no man regarded; but ye have set at nought all my counsel, and would none of my reproof: I also will laugh at your calamity . . . Then shall they call upon me, but I will not answer; they shall seek me early, but they shall not find me: for that they hated knowledge, and did not choose the fear of the Lord . . . (Proverbs 1:24–30).

Added light increases guilt, verse 24 implies. The more we know of the truth, the more sermons we hear, the deeper the conviction of the Holy Spirit; and the more our conscience is awakened, the guiltier we become before God. The greater will be our judgment. Enlightenment leaves us without excuse.

It is a most serious sin to spurn God's love, to reject His

Son, whom He gave as a sacrifice for our sins, and to spurn the salvation which He bought at such a mighty price—the price of His blood. God does not feel kindly toward such refusal (verse 24).

Sin brings its own retribution, and when the grief it causes falls upon you, if you have refused God's love, your cries for help will fall upon deaf ears (verses 25–26). Once the judgment falls it will be too late to repent.

A twenty-nine-year-old mother of five children was rushed to the hospital in very serious condition. She was dying, bleeding internally due to sclerosis of the liver, caused by too much drink. Her husband sent for the minister and pled, "Please pray for her! She's dying! Ask God to save her!"

"It is too late to pray for her now," the minister replied. "Irreparable damage has already been done. Repentance is now too late!"

What a tragedy! This is exactly what verses 25–28 mean. The rich man in hell repented, but it was too late. Once sin comes to fruition it is too late to escape its penalty (verse 28).

Those who spurn salvation and reject Christ will eventually come to ruin. They will be able to blame only themselves. God does not want any man to perish. He has put the cross between every man and hell; if a person goes to hell, it will be in spite of all that God has done to save him, and it will be his own fault.

SIN BRINGS ITS OWN RETRIBUTION

Therefore shall they eat of the fruit of their own way, and be filled with their own devices. . . . Whoso hearkeneth unto me shall dwell safely . . . (Proverbs 1:31–33).

The wages of sin is death, and sin always pays its wages! Sin always bears fruit. Shake the tree and rid it of its fruit before it ripens! Otherwise it will be too late. The sinner is apt to take it easy and to remain content, continuing in sin, but his spiritual indolence will end in sudden destruction (verse 32).

However, God offers the sinner a safe dwelling place if he will repent and turn to Christ. He will then dwell in peace and quiet, with freedom from fear of eternal judgment (verse 33).

The Quest for Knowledge

Proverbs 2:1–5

If thou seekest her as silver, and searchest for her as for hid treasures; then shalt thou understand the fear of the Lord, and find the knowledge of God. (Proverbs 2: 4, 5).

Knowledge is more valuable than gold or precious gems. It is life's richest treasure. We should search for it with the same zeal that a prospector searches for gold. Knowledge is not discovered through wishful thinking, nor through some magic formula. We are not born with it. Knowledge is gained through untiring effort and tedious searching or study. The ignorant may envy the wise, but they, too, could be wise if they were willing to pay the price. Those who are not as mentally keen as some others may find that knowledge must be gained through more effort and with greater difficulty, but all may gain knowledge if they seek it.

All knowledge is valuable, but knowledge concerning spiritual things is far superior to secular knowledge. A young streetcar motorman was so fascinated with divine knowledge when he was saved that he spent most of the night studying his Bible until his eyes closed from weariness. At times he would return to work without having had one hour of sleep, so fascinated was he with God's Word. Soon he devoted his entire life to the Word and became a great preacher of the gospel.

Notice the progression of conquest for the truth as related in Proverbs 2:1–5: (1) We receive. (2) We hide His commandments. (3) We apply His truth. (4) We cry after truth. (5) We seek knowledge as silver. (6) We understand the fear of the Lord, or comprehend true reverence. (7) The great discovery is made—we find the knowledge of the Lord.

Too many Christians are spiritually weak and emaciated,

19

because they lack spiritual knowledge. They are not willing to pay the price of seeking the truth. Study is tedious for them, and they are lazy. We are admonished: "Study to shew thyself approved unto God" (II Timothy 2:15).

Knowledge becomes valuable only when it is applied (verse 2). It is useless to study the Word of God and then not to apply it to our daily lives. Knowledge must be translated into action. James warned, "Be ye doers of the word, and not hearers only, deceiving your own selves" (James 1:22).

KNOWLEDGE THROUGH DIVINE REVELATION

Proverbs 2:6–9

For the Lord giveth wisdom: out of his mouth cometh knowledge and understanding.—Proverbs 2:6

Knowledge and truth are gained through personal experience or through divine revelation. A scientist examines what God has made, then he accumulates facts, records these facts in order and preserves them. Scientific knowledge, we may conclude, is limited to materialism in this world and cannot go beyond the record of the rocks, the archives of history, and the forces of nature which are now in action. Processes of creation have long since ended according to Genesis 2:2; therefore the processes of creation are hidden from the true scientist, for they are nonexistent today. Future events are equally a mystery to him, for no evidence yet exists concerning the hereafter. Death is a great enigma to the scientist.

Likewise, the philosopher also depends upon human reason. Human reason is limited and therefore prone to error. He can only guess as to the ages before creation, and he can only conjecture as to the future. His opinions are not deductions from basic truth; he must rely upon his own reason.

But God did not make us creatures of reason and then leave us in total darkness as to the ages past, or without knowledge as to the ages to come. Through divine revelation he has made known unto us both the past and the future.

Divine revelation comes to us in two ways: either through the person of Jesus Christ, who is God manifest in the flesh (See John 1:14 and 18), or else through the inspired Word of God (See I Peter 1:10–12).

That the Bible is a divine revelation of God is self-evident. No man can foretell the future; this is a capability limited to deity, and omniscience is one of the attributes of deity. The Bible does foretell the future; therefore the source of this knowledge must be God. The Bible is not a book of science, and yet it is scientifically accurate. Even in our day of advanced scientific knowledge, Scriptures which were written four thousand years ago are in agreement with proven scientific truth. Though it is not a book of history, yet God prophetically foretold facts before they happened more accurately at times than historians recorded the events after they had transpired!

The Bible is the source of vital information related to all spiritual truths, and also the secrets of successful living are revealed therein. The Bible is the foundation for all law and morality, guiding us into the paths of human relationships which are essential for our happiness and peace of mind. It contains the secrets of a happy, fruitful life.

KNOWLEDGE IS A REWARD

Proverbs 2:10–22

When wisdom entereth into thine heart, and knowledge is pleasant unto thy soul; discretion shall preserve thee, understanding shall keep thee.—(Proverbs 2:10–11).

Knowledge is its own reward. Those who have it find the answer to the cry of their soul. It brings peace and satisfaction.

The reward of knowledge is threefold according to Proverbs 2:10–22. First, it delivers us from the way of the evil man. Isaiah wrote: *All we like sheep have gone astray* (Isaiah 53:6). As a nation we go astray together. As members of society we go astray together. If we associate with evil men we will go astray with them. We sin because we "follow the crowd"!

We may guard against being misled through knowledge of the Word of God. Christ is the Way, the Truth, and the Life! (See John 14:6).

Second, we are delivered from temptation of the wicked woman, and the temptations of sexual sin, through a knowledge of the Word of God. "An ounce of prevention is worth a pound of cure." Those who are tempted into sexual sin seldom return to a life of morality (verse 19). David wrote: "Thy Word have I hid in mine heart, that I might not sin against thee" (Psalm 119:11).

Third, Bible knowledge brings a life of peace and security (verse 21). But the wicked are soon cut off. Their life is brief and unrewarding (verse 22).

Three Things to Remember

REMEMBER GOD'S LAW

Proverbs 3:1, 2

My son, forget not my law; but let thine heart keep my commandments: for length of days, and long life, and peace, shall they add to thee.—Proverbs 3:1, 2

Some years ago, a minister's health was breaking. His physician gave him a prescription for medicine which he promised would cure him. "Take your medicine faithfully every day, and you will be a well man," the physician said.

The minister put the prescription in his pocket and immediately went to the drug store to have the prescription filled. The druggist looked at the prescription and smiled. "Sorry," he said, "but I cannot fill this prescription. You will have to do that yourself!"

The druggist handed the prescription back to he minister, who looked at it for the first time. Slowly he read it: "Read the book of Proverbs every day and do what it says."

The minister smiled, returned home and started to read Proverbs. When he came to Proverbs 2:1, 2, he asked himself, "Why have I ignored this advice all my life?"

God promises added days and peace to those who will obey His commandments.

Sin collects a heavy toll from those who ignore the commands of God. It has been estimated that a heavy smoker may deduct ten year from his life.* A heart specialist has estimated that heart attacks are caused more from worry than by any other cause. Those who have faith in God, who commit their problems to the Lord, enjoy better health than do others.

An Austrian physician has devoted his entire life to the study of glandular activity of the body. He has concluded

* *Reader's Digest*, page 147, August, 1973—*Harper's Magazine*, June, 1973

that hate, fear, anger, and worry cause an imbalance in the glandular activity of the body, leading to an upset in the metabolism, resulting at last in a complete breakdown in health.

When you purchase any machine or gadget, the manufacturer furnishes you with directions for the operation and care of the product. To ignore these directions is to invite trouble. And to ignore the laws of God is to invite an early grave. Your Maker has given you directions in the Bible for successful and healthy living.

Not only does God promise long life if we obey His commandments, He also promises that our days will be more rewarding. In other words, you will receive the most out of life if you obey God. Life has purpose and meaning when we live for Christ. Paul said, "For to me to live is Christ" (Philippians 1:21).

Even more precious to the obedient Christian is the reward of peace. Doctors do not know the actual cause of kidney stones, or gall stones, but some think that they are the result of worry and strain. It is thought ulcers are caused by worry and nervous tension. Therefore peace becomes a most valuable asset for good health. Peace is found only when we obey God. Faith in God delivers us from guilt. But there is no peace for the law breaker.

Peace results from inner contentment, and it is not to be found from environment. The world in which you dwell may be in a turmoil, but if Christ abides within your heart, He will impart peace and assurance to you. He will guide you and lead you beside the still waters. He will anoint your head with oil and give you water to drink in the presence of your enemies.

A famous artist searched nature for a picture that would portray peace. He came to a waterfall just as a storm was darkening the earth. He hid in a cave and watched a robin sitting in her nest with her young quietly waiting for the storm to pass. The wind whipped spray from the water falls upon the nest, and the limb of the tree whipped in the gale. Overhead, lightning spit from cloud to cloud, and thunder shook the earth. Black clouds glared upon the scene.

Quickly the artist sketched the scene and hastened to his studio to capture its mood upon canvas. When he had finished his work of art, he captioned it, *Peace*.

When the sun is shining, when all goes well, it is not difficult to have peace, but peace in the midst of trouble is a gift from God. Those who know this peace enjoy health and long life.

Jesus' bequest to His disciples just before He left this earth was: "My peace I give unto you: not as the world giveth, give I unto you. Let not your heart be troubled, neither let it be afraid." (John 14:27).

REMEMBER MERCY

Let not mercy and truth forsake thee: bind them about thy neck; write them upon the table of thine heart: so shalt thou find favour and good understanding in the sight of God and man.—Proverbs 3:3–4

Mercy is not to be confused with justice. A man awaiting trial in court was extremely nervous. The judge, upon noticing his fright said, "You need not be afraid, Sir. This court will give you justice."

The defendant replied, "That's just the thing I fear. What I need, your honor, is not justice, but mercy, for I am guilty."

As guilty sinners, we all need to plead guilty, and to throw ourselves upon the mercy of God. We need forgiveness. God's mercy is extended to us through the death of His Son, Jesus Christ, upon the cross, Who met the requirements of divine justice in our behalf and now offers to us His mercy. "By grace are ye saved through faith; and that not of yourselves: it is the gift of God: not of works, lest any man should boast" (Ephesians 2:8, 9).

Inasmuch as we have received mercy from God, should we not show mercy to others?

A minister was greatly disturbed by the actions of a trouble-maker in his church. His patience was almost exhausted, when he learned from a psychiatrist that the person who was causing so much trouble was suffering from an inner conflict. Immediately he sought to help this person overcome her personal problems, rather than to reprimand her for her failures. A reprimand would have made her condition more serious. By showing her understanding and mercy, he helped her.

The Good Samaritan showed mercy to his enemy. He did not allow racial bias or prejudice to interfere with his acts of kindness. God is well pleased with those who show mercy.

Christ told a parable of a man who was greatly in debt,

but was forgiven. Immediately he cast into prison one who was indebted to him refusing to show mercy. Wereupon mercy was withdrawn from him! Shall we accept the mercy of God in the forgiveness of sins, and then refuse to show mercy to others?

If we please men, we will also please God. Those who are at peace with God are also at peace with fellowmen. The two always go together.

REMEMBER TRUTH

Let not mercy and truth forsake thee—Proverbs 3:3

We should wear both mercy and truth about our necks as an adorning necklace.

Truth should guard us against all falsehood, lies, hypocrisy; and most assuredly God disdains a person who makes a false profession. Both God and men see through the subterfuge of the false and dishonest person. The hypocrite deceives only himself, and he does more harm than good when he makes a profession that he is a Christian when actually he is false. Our lives should support the testimony of our lips. Only then will we find favor with God and man.

Three Worthwhile Admonitions

Trust in the Lord with all thine heart; and lean not unto thine own understanding. In all thy ways acknowledge him, and he shall direct thy paths.—Proverbs 3:5, 6

Self confidence, assurance and peace begin with trust in God. Worry is the chief cause of mental illness, nervousness, and unhappiness. We live in a day of trouble, turmoil, and uncertainty. People are confused and do not know which way to turn.

Our forefathers also faced serious dangers. Early settlers faced possible death and starvation. Wars have always scourged the earth. Despots in their ambition for power and wealth have tormented men, women, and children. Criminals have always threatened the security and well-being of people. But in the past, people endured these troubles and lived more victoriously than we do today. Why?

Our present generation is turning to drink, dope, and tranquilizers. People seek to quench their cares with pleasures and entertainment in a desperate desire to overcome their fears and trials. In contrast, our forefathers, who had learned the true secret of happiness and contentment, trusted in the Lord. They went regularly to the House of the Lord where they found the answer to their troubles. They overcame Satan and his wiles through the armor of the Christian. Faith, prayer, love, and worship supplied them with the strength for the day. Today, however, multitudes have forsaken the church, the Bible, and prayer.

The word *trust* means to commit self unto God for salvation, protection, and power. To trust is to fall into His arms and to rest in Him completely. We cease to struggle when we trust. Let us illustrate: We may look at a chair and believe that it is capable of holding us, but not until we sit in that chair and rest ourselves completely upon it, do we trust

27

in it. That is what the Bible means when it says, "Believe on the Lord Jesus Christ and thou shalt be saved." Trust in the Lord! Trust is the cure for all of your worries and troubles. Do not allow circumstances to overcome your spirit and cause you to despair.

We are to trust in the Lord with all of our heart. The heart is the center of emotions and affection. To trust with all our heart is to have confidence in the Lord because we love Him, obey Him, and know that He will not fail.

The world is dependent upon human reason in solving problems. The Christian has this advantage: He seeks guidance from God, Who foreknows the future. God knows all, and His will for us is always best. God loves us and will not allow us to suffer anything which is not for our good. Furthermore, there is nothing impossible with God. Therefore, we may trust Him implicitly, knowing that what is best, He will do. On the other hand, we can never be sure of human reasoning. We make wrong choices because of human limitations.

Jesus meant just that when He said to His disciples, "Let not your heart be troubled, ye believe in God, believe also in me." They did already believe in the deity of Christ. What then did Christ mean? He meant they were to trust Him even when they saw Him hanging on a cross. They were to believe even though they could not understand the course of events. They were not to doubt His love. Let us likewise trust God even when we cannot understand, knowing that He will always love us and do what is best for us.

Faith requires us to acknowledge God in all our ways. He will make our path and our future clear before us. He will guide us with His eye. Accept whatever comes to pass as His will. (See I Thessalonians 5:18).

BE GOD-DEPENDENT—NOT SELF-DEPENDENT

Be not wise in thine own eyes: fear the Lord, and depart from evil. It shall be health to thy navel, and marrow to thy bones.—Proverbs 3:7, 8.

The wayward and sinful man is self-satisfied. He is proud and arrogant. He says, "I can get along without God!" But at the same time he is using what God has given him—he breathes God's air, drinks His water, and eats His food. His very breath is in the hands of God. He isn't getting along without God, but God is getting along without him!

The sinner forgets God until the day of trouble, then he either cries to God for help, or else he gives up, despairs of life itself. Suicide is often his way out. Isaiah warns. "Seek ye the Lord while he may be found, call ye upon him while he is near" (Isaiah 55:6).

To trust God and acknowledge His sovereignty and our need of Him is to enjoy health and happiness. Proverbs 3:8 implies a cure for nervous disorder. Blood is manufactured in the marrow of the bones. Thus life and health are dependent upon our trust in God.

During World War I, two American soldiers who had grown up together in the same community fought side by side on the battlefield, seeing the same horrible sights, and sharing in the same horrors of war. The one young man went through the war unscathed and unharmed. The other boy went insane! The psychiatrist sought to discover what the difference was between the two boys. They found that the one boy was a Christian, but the other was not. That was the only difference! Faith in God is essential to a sound mind.

BE GENEROUS

Honour the Lord with thy substance, and with the first-fruits of all thine increase: so shall thy barns be filled with plenty, and thy presses shall burst out with new wine.—Proverbs 3:9, 10.

God's Word teaches both tithing and stewardship. As stewards, we are servants entrusted with the Lord's possessions. As tithers, we pay rent to God for the use of His creation. Someday we will be called upon to give an accounting to the Lord for every dollar we have spent. At the Bema Judgment we will be rewarded according to our faithfulness.

We are commanded to bring our tithes into God's storehouse the first day of every week: "Upon the first day of the week let every one of you lay by him in store, as God hath prospered him" (I Corinthians 16:2). Leviticus 27:30 commands: "All the tithe of the land, whether of the seed of the land, or of the fruit of the tree, is the Lord's: it is holy unto the Lord."

Some would excuse themselves from tithing by arguing that the tithe applies only to those who were under the Old Testament Covenant of the Law. But Jacob paid a tithe before the Covenant of the Law was ever given. (See Genesis 28:22). And so did Abraham, the father of the Hebrews, pay a tithe to Melchizedek, whom many theologians consider to be Christ. (See Genesis 14:20). Tithing is referred to in the New Testament in Hebrews 7:1–10. Should we not do as much or even more while living under the Covenant of Grace, as Old Testament saints did under the Covenant of the Law? Tithing is the Biblical method of giving. But let us remember, that after we have tithed, as stewards, we must still answer to God for faithful handling of the remaining ninety percent of our wealth, for we ourselves, and all we possess, belong to God!

God's promise is clear: "Give, and it shall be given unto you."

Blessing in Chastisement

CHASTENING IS FOR CORRECTION

My son, despise not the chastening of the Lord; neither be weary of his correction.—Proverbs 3:11

Job said, "Surely it is meet to be said unto God, I have borne chastisement, I will not offend any more: That which I see not teach thou me: if I have done iniquity, I will do no more" (Job 34:31, 32). A child of God wishes to do right. He wishes to please God and he desires to avoid evil at any cost. If chastisement is an aid to right living, the sincere Christian yearns for such correction.

A young father said to his own father, "Father, I want to thank you for every whipping you ever gave me. I am grateful for every rebuke you gave me for wrong doing. You were a faithful father, and as a father I now know that it wasn't pleasant for you to punish me. But I am a successful man today because you did not spare the rod when I was a boy."

The parent who fails to punish a child who does wrong is not being kind to that child. Kindness is to discipline a child and to teach him right from wrong. The ability to cope with the temptations and trials of the world depends upon early training. Character develops through trial.

Discipline saves us from much sorrow and tragedy. A child would put his hand on a red hot stove if the parent did not warn him and stop him. Some believe that a child should be allowed to develop his own character without correction, to encourage initiative in the child. But is it not better for a child to learn the right way through instruction and chastisement rather than through mistakes? Is it not wise to profit from the experiences of others?

Let us then be grateful for both the chastening of our earthly parents and for the chastening of our Heavenly Father. Chastening is the school of success.

31

CHASTENING IS AN ACT OF LOVE

For whom the Lord loveth he correcteth; even as a father the son in whom he delighteth.—Proverbs 3:12

Hebrews 12:3–15 is an enlargement upon Proverbs 3:11, 12. We suggest that you compare these passages carefully.

Hebrews 12:6 repeats, "Whom the Lord loveth he chasteneth, and scourgeth every son whom he receiveth." None of us is immune to suffering. We must all go through our Gethsemane sooner or later.

Most of us squirm and complain when we are going through the fires of chastening. Some even complain, saying, "God doesn't love me, else He would not allow me to suffer so much."

A professor at Columbia University once asked, "Would you wish for your children to suffer?" He answered his own question by saying, "Of course not! Then God would not want any of His children to suffer. Therefore, He will always heal the sick who ask Him for healing."

I replied, "Sir, if one of my children had appendicitis, I would most assuredly want him to suffer the pain of the knife on the operating table. For it is better to suffer than to die. Likewise, there are times when God puts us through the fires of trial and suffering to refine our character and to make us what we ought to be. Sickness may be one chastening which God permits, to build our character, and to teach us to trust and pray."

Trials reveal our weaknesses and faults. They show us where and how we may improve. They force us to seek the help of the Lord in correcting character flaws.

A tree roots deep when it faces heavy winds and endures much drought. Even so, a Christian will root deeply in Christ if he endures much trial and testing. Great characters are made in the fires of trial.

Furthermore, trials drive us to our knees to seek the face of God. God answers our prayers and reveals His greatness, His love, and His goodness. We learn to know Him better in the hour of our trial. Our faith would remain weak if we did not go to Him in our hour of need and learn that God does answer prayer.

God keeps us in the fires of trial until He can see the beauty of His face reflected in us. We must be like Him.

CHASTENING IS A FATHER-SON RELATIONSHIP

For whom the Lord loveth he correcteth; even as a father the son in whom he delighteth.—Proverbs 3:12

Some years ago, my son, five years of age, decided he would run away from home. He didn't go far—only a half of a block, where he talked to the man at the filling station, who warned him it would soon be dark, and he would have no place to sleep. So he returned home.

As he started up the front steps to the house, I tapped him lightly on the seat of his pants and scolded him for running away. That light spanking made him feel much better, because it was evidence that he was still a member of the family! It really felt good! So it is with Christians. Chastisement is proof that we are sons of God. Those who can sin and not be chastened are not really sons of God. (Read Hebrews 12:8).

Fatherly rebuke makes us fruitful (See John 15:1–8).

Fatherly rebuke assures us of a future reward at the Bema Judgment of Christ. (See Hebrews 12:10–15).

Fatherly rebuke is sent from God for our own blessing and good. (See Deuteronomy 8:15, 16; 11:2, 3).

Life's Greatest Discovery

To Find Christ is to Find Life

(Proverbs 3:13–18)

Happy is the man that findeth wisdom . . . She is a tree of life to them that lay hold upon her.—Proverbs 3:13, 18.

A young preacher, sixteen years of age, had just finished his message, when a young lady approached him and said, "I feel sorry for you. You can't have a good time like the rest of us young people. You're a Christian, and you don't dare do anything that's fun, do you?"

"I'm afraid you have it backwards," the young preacher replied. "You don't know what true happiness is. Not until you find Christ as your Saviour will you begin to really enjoy life. Happiness and fullness of life are not realized until you are born again."

"Happy is the man that findeth wisdom!" And wisdom is Jesus Christ. Jesus said, I am the way, *the truth,* and the life" (John 14:6). Colossians 2:3 says of Christ Jesus, "In whom are hid all the treasures of wisdom and knowledge."

The devil misleads people into thinking that there is no happiness in the Christian life; actually the very opposite is true. The happy man is the man in Christ. He is described in Psalm I as the blessed man.

Does Christ dwell within your heart? If so, He brings His joy and sunshine into your soul. Jesus said to the woman at the well, "Whosoever drinketh of the water that I shall give him shall never thirst; but the water that I shall give him shall be in him a well of water springing up into everlasting life" (John 4:14). Friend, drink of the waters of life and be satisfied!"

Christ is to be preferred to silver and gold or any other earthly treasure. Yet many people make the mistake of choos-

34

ing money instead of Christ; they have made money their god.

Christ is a greater treasure than rubies, the most rare and expensive of precious gems. Christ brings more pleasure and joy. He is everlasting; He abides with you forever. Moses chose Christ above all the treasures and wealth of Egypt. (See Hebrews 11:25, 26). By faith he foresaw a better day—the day of reward, and he chose to reign with Christ for eternity, rather than to enjoy a few short years of pleasure on this earth, during a brief lifetime.

Christ is more precious than your fondest ambition or your deepest desire (Proverbs 3:15).

To have Christ is to enjoy a full and long life (Proverbs 3:16). Long life brings with it riches and honor. Jesus said, "Seek ye first the kingdom of God, and his righteousness; and all these things shall be added unto you" (Matthew 6:33). Thus we are assured clothing, food, and material wealth, for Christ was referring to these when He said, "all things."

The Christian life is a pleasant life, and the path of a Christian is the way of peace. It pays to walk in the "Jesus Way," as the American Indians call it (Proverbs 3:17).

Ponce de Leon searched the world, hoping to find the tree of life, or the waters of everlasting life. But the Christian has discovered this fountain of life! He has found a tree that bears the fruit eternal life (Proverbs 3:18).

To Find Christ is to Find the Answer to Creation

The Lord by wisdom hath founded the earth; by understanding hath he established the heavens. By his knowledge the depths are broken up, and the clouds drop down the dew.—Proverbs 3:19, 20

The man without Christ is deceived by many wild and foolish ideas concerning the source of creation and life. Scientific fact states that mass and life cannot be created by man. Nor can creation be destroyed by man. Those who are without God cannot explain life or creation, so they claim that it came by accident. How foolish it is to assume that the atom just happened, or that life just happened. The careful design and the intricate laws of creation and life testify to the fact that they were planned by a great mind. The lower order of animals do not have the power to think, to bring about progress in their own development. In other words, man could not have made himself. The power to think, the circulatory system, the reproduction system, the personality, and the soul of man were carefully planned and designed. Evolution is a farce! The theory that the world developed from gaseous particles by accident is ridiculous! Who created the force that holds the sea in its place? Who planned the orbits of the stars and holds them there? Certainly it did not happen by chance. A great mind planned it all.

Those who have found Christ and know Him have discovered the key that unlocks the riddle of creation and life. Christ demonstrated His power of life and creation when He arose from the grave. Proverbs 3:19, 20 asserts that creation was brought into being by the mind of Christ. John 1:3, 4; Colossians 1:15–17; Hebrews 1:2, 10, all agree with this great truth.

To Find Christ is to Find Deliverance From Fear

(Proverbs 3:21–26)

When thou liest down, thou shalt not be afraid . . . Be not afraid of sudden fear . . . For the Lord shall be thy confidence, and shall keep thy foot from being taken.—Proverbs 3:24–26

Fear hounds the footsteps of most people today. It is destroying the joy of life and causing much mental illness. Those who find Christ find deliverance from all fear, no matter what may be the cause.

God guides the steps of the Christian, and keeps him in all his ways. He leads him in paths of righteousness (Proverbs 3:23). He keeps him from stumbling. On the other hand, the sinner walks in slippery places and falls into temptation and crime. His life is filled with violence and sorrow.

God's child sleeps in peace, free from fear, for he commits his life into God's care and keeping (Proverbs 3:24). "He will not suffer thy foot to be moved: he that keepeth thee will not slumber. Behold, he that keepeth Israel shall neither slumber nor sleep. The Lord is thy keeper: the Lord is thy shade upon thy right hand" (Psalm 121:3–5).

Why should we stay awake and worry? Sudden catastrophe should not worry the Christian, for God keeps us under all circumstances (Proverbs 3:25). The Lord is our confidence. Jesus never fails; He will always protect His children (Proverbs 3:26).

Let Us Do Good

GOODNESS CAN BE NEGATIVE

Withhold not good from them to who it is due, when it is in the power of thine hand to do it. Say not unto thy neighbor, Go, and come again, and tomorrow I will give; when thou hast it by thee.—Proverbs 3:27, 28

Did you ever hear a person boast of his "negative goodness" during a church testimony meeting? "I don't drink. I don't swear. I don't lie. I don't cheat. I don't steal. I don't smoke." On and on he continues boasting about what he does not do. They seem to think that righteousness is a negative vacuum. But God is not so much interested in what we do not do as in what we do do! Goodness is positive. Too many Christians are good, but good for nothing! They never bear witness for Christ. They have no concern for the poor. They refuse to sing in the choir. They will not teach a Sunday School class, though they are capable. They never win a soul to Christ. They do not comfort the broken-hearted. It is questionable as to what goodness they do.

Our text tells us we are to do good when it is in our power to do so. Failure to do good is a sin. If we see a man in need and refuse to give him food when we could, we have sinned by default. James said, "If a brother or sister be naked, and destitute of daily food, and one of you say unto them, Depart in peace, be ye warmed and filled; notwithstanding ye give them not those things which are needful to the body; what doth it profit?" (James 2:15, 16).

A hungry man once asked a Christian for food. "No," the Christian replied. "I will not give you food. If you were a Christian you would not be in trouble. If you will accept Christ, then I will buy you a dinner."

The hungry man replied, "If you weren't so religious, maybe you would be more charitable. How can I listen to what you say when your actions prove that your heart is without sympathy?"

37

Remember to do good when it is in your power to do so.

Secondly, never be dishonest in an attempt to get out of doing good. A mother in Cleveland, Ohio, took her little boy shopping in a department store. She stopped to look at some jewelry. "May I see that ring?" she asked.

"Certainly," the clerk replied. Finally he asked as she admired the item, "Madam, would you like to buy this ring?"

"Not today, thank you," she said. "Some other time."

The little boy looked up at his mother and asked, "Mommy, when do you plan to buy it?"

"Shhhh," she whispered. "That was only an excuse. I don't intend to ever buy it."

She had lied, and her little boy knew it. In a similar way so many people lie to God, promising to serve Him later, when they have no intention of fulfilling their promise. They make a vow with the Lord, covenanting to give, or to serve the Lord, if He will help them in a time of dire need. But when God answers their cry and delivers them out of their troubles, or else blesses them in a singular way, they soon forget their promise. This is nothing but hypocrisy.

THOU SHALL NOT

Withhold not good . . . Say not unto thy neighbor, Go and come again . . . Devise not evil . . . Strive not . . . Envy thou not . . . choose none of his ways.—Proverbs 3:27–31

On the other hand, righteousness may consist in our refusal to do evil against another brother. Note that there are five commandments in Proverbs 3:27–31, and all five are negative. The ten commandments are negative. They warn us against doing wrong.

We have already discussed the first two commandments in our text. The third, "Devise not evil against thy neighbor," implies that we are not to plan trouble for our neighbor. Recently a woman was suffering a serious psychological conflict which was so serious she had to be hospitalized. The psychiatrist discovered that the cause of her problem was a neighbor who deliberately devised schemes to annoy and trouble this woman. It is tragic when Christians plot trouble against others in order to seek vengeance.

The fourth "thou-shalt-not" is, "Strive not with a man without cause." Some people carry a chip on their shoulder. They are always in a conflict with others. They are constantly in court, defending themselves. The motive behind such a quarrelsome attitude usually is the desire to be important—to dominate. Self is all-important to such people, and they are always complaining of being hurt or harmed, when no harm is intended. This is a serious personal problem which such a person should earnestly seek to overcome.

The fifth "thou-shalt-not" is, "Envy thou not the oppressor." Many envy the success of evil men. We must learn that happiness is not the product of environment. Happiness is a state of mind and heart. Therefore, take your eyes off the sinner and make sure you are at peace with God.

GOD REWARDS BOTH EVIL AND GOOD

(Proverbs 3:32–35)

The curse of the Lord is in the house of the wicked: but he blesseth the habitation of the just.—Proverbs 3: 33

God disdains the rebellious person, who refuses to obey or to yield to the right. God takes the righteous man into confidence and reveals His secrets. He curses the sinner, but He blesses the righteous. God scorns the critical, but He loves the lowly and the good. He gives glory to the righteous, but shame to the fools.

The Path of the Just

The path of the just is as the shining light, that shineth more and more unto the perfect day.—Proverbs 4:18

As A Shining Light

What does the future hold? Which way shall I go? What is right, and what is wrong? These questions may be summed up with the expression, "The way I shall walk." The people of the world have lost their way. They are stumbling in darkness. Their path is uncertain, and the future is unknown. They do not know which way to turn, and they are confused. In answer to this uncertainty, we hear Christ saying, "I am the way."

The Christian no longer walks in darkness. Life has taken on a new glow, and the path is clear. He is following Jesus, and he never walks alone. Even when he walks through the valley of the shadow of death, he need fear no evil, for Christ has promised to go with him. The Master has walked this pathway before. He has gone through death and has come out into the sunlight of life after death.

The Christian has the Holy Spirit dwelling within his heart as his guide and comforter (John 14:16–18). There can be no uncertainty nor loneliness when He is our constant companion. A mission superintendent asked a young Christian, "Where is the Holy Spirit?"

"He's in my heart," the young man replied.

"Could He be any closer than that?" asked the mission worker. If you are a child of God, He dwells within you. What a glorious truth!

Life to the unsaved person often grows darker and darker, until eventually he may despair, sometimes committing suicide. But the Christian has found the way of life. He walks down a path of sunshine, and his life is filled with joy. The unrest of the unsaved is reflected in the riots and turmoil in the city streets. If only these dissatisfied and disillusioned ones knew Christ, life would take on a new and glorious light for them.

Christ is the Light of the World (John 1:5–9). Light symbolizes righteousness in contrast with sin. It illustrates faith in contrast with the darkness of unbelief and skepticism. To know Christ is to trust Him. Light is fellowship with God. Those living in darkness are in rebellion against Him. John 1:5 has been aptly translated, "The Light continues to pierce the darkness, for the darkness has never been able to put out, or extinguish, the light." This implies that right finally will win against darkness. It assures us that if we know Christ and are righteous, we are on the winning side!

In John 3:19, 20, darkness illustrates the sin of the unsaved man in contrast with the light of righteousness. The unsaved man is in darkness because his deeds are evil and he wishes to hide them. He has a sense of guilt.

In John 9:5 Christ said that He is the Light of the World. He can heal our spiritual blindness.

In Revelation 21:23, 24, Christ is the Light of Heaven! Those who dwell in heaven dwell and walk forever in His light. There is no darkness or sin whatsoever in heaven. It is sin on earth that causes men to stumble in darkness.

Who is the just man mentioned in our text? He is the man made righteous through faith in Jesus Christ. He has been washed and cleansed in the blood of Christ. He is not only just before God; he is also just in his dealings with other men. He is fair and honest. His life is blessed, and his path is clear and lighted with the presence of the Lord.

IT SHINETH MORE AND MORE

The Christian life and walk grow better and better. The light of His blessing increases every day. Life grows sweeter each step of the way. The sinner's way grows darker each day, and as he nears death and eternity, he stumbles the more. Fear grips his heart.

The Christian's walk brings him nearer home, until finally the light of heaven falls upon his pathway. Rewards accumulate, and experience deepens until his life is mature in Christ and he is prepared to walk the streets of heaven. Romans 5:1–5 lists the steps of the spiritual growth that take the Christian into the presence of God. The mature Christian is one who has grown through tests, trials, and tribulation.

THAT PERFECT DAY

Out text implies that as the sun rises in the morning and dawn breaks, the day of eternal life begins. As the day continues, the light increases, until noon brings full light and glory to the day. So is the Christian life. It begins with the low light of dawn, when we accept Christ as our Saviour, but the light and glory increase until we reach the perfect day—heaven itself!

Death brings ruin and judgment to the sinner, but death ushers the Christian into the glorious presence of Christ (II Corinthians 5:8). There we will walk the streets of gold. We have an eternal home awaiting us in heaven (John 14:1-3; Hebrews 11:10, 15-16). Death brings us to an end of sin, sorrow, and suffering. Death brings us into the presence of our Lord Jesus Christ and our loved ones.

Finally, the perfect day will restore our loved ones to us in resurrection glory (I Thessalonians 4:13-18). As Jesus said, we will enter into "the more abundant life" (John 10:10). Our life is bright today, but the best is yet to come!

Warning Against Sexual Sin

For the lips of a strange woman drop as an honey-
comb, and her mouth is smoother than oil: but her end
is bitter as wormwood, sharp as a twoedged sword. Her
feet go down to death; her steps take hold on hell.
—Proverbs 5:3–5

Sex is not sin. Sex abused or misused is sin. God created sex, but lust is the result of the fall of man. Love makes sex blessed. Lust reduces sex to immorality.

Paganism made a religion of sexual abuse. It dealt in immorality and adultery as a part of its worship. The New Testament epistles have much to say about the sexual abuse under paganism, and today we have reverted to the same debasement of sin which the pagans practiced. To many people sex has ceased to be an expression of love. It has become an experience of lust in search for pleasure. It is a most disappointing and unsatisfactory experience for those who have abused its purpose and meaning.

Sex is an integral part of marriage, the home, and love. Change its natural purpose and it becomes sin, imparting a deep sense of guilt, enslaving those who worship at its shrine of corruption. Much mental illness and disappointment, leading to suicide, results from the pagan abuse of sex.

Temptation is so subtle. The forbidden fruit appears to be so pleasant (verse 3). Experimentation is all a part of temptation. As Satan tempted Eve to taste and see that the fruit of sin was pleasant, her inquisitive nature responded to the enticement. So many fall into sexual sin when a desire to experiment and partake of the untasted fruit overcomes them. The actual experience of lust is most devastating and disappointing. Once indulged in, a person easily becomes enslaved, and as Adam's and Eve's eyes were opened in disappointment, the sinner wishes he or she had never tasted of the forbidden fruit.

43

The sinner thinks only of the momentary pleasures of the flesh, and is so overcome that he ceases to use reason (verses 4, 5). He fails to consider the ultimate end of his deed, and the consequences of what will surely follow.

We are living in days when pre-marital sex experience is common-place, because the fear of unwanted children has been removed by science. However, there are many other dangers which are far more serious which should be considered. The end of sexual sin is death and hell, Proverbs warns. Many there are who have fled from the presence of God, ashamed to confess their sin and seek forgiveness.

The sexual sinner lives carelessly, thinking only of the moment, not caring what the future may hold (verse 6). The sinner doesn't worry about the future. He thinks only of one thing: *I must satisfy the strong urge of sex, and nothing else matters.* Shame, disgrace, loss of reputation, loss of a job or position, broken and disappointed hearts of those who have loved and trusted us often are the result. Be sure your sins will find you out. Also be sure that the wages of sin is death. Sin always pays wages!

The best way to avoid sexual sin is to avoid temptation (verse 8). "Blessed is the man that walketh not in the counsel of the ungodly" (Psalm 1:1). It is easier to avoid temptation than it is to overcome it. No man can be sure of himself, and all should avoid whatever may lead to sin, whether it be reading pornographical literature, viewing lustful movies, or keeping company with dissolute characters. Many have fallen because they overestimated their ability to withstand temptation. Avoid it! Sin begins with carelessness.

There is another great danger which accompanies sexual sin—blackmail. Why should you put yourself in the position of danger which a moment of sexual illicit pleasure may grant you, when you know that it may impoverish you the remainder of your life? Many a sorry person has spent years in prison for a moment of satisfaction of lust (verses 9–11).

The sexual sinner will eventually regret the fact that advice was spurned (verses 12, 13).

The loss of reputation as a result of sexual sin is most certain. Such sin almost always becomes known, and the public does not respect such a person (verse 14). Consider the serious consequences for a moment of false pleasure.

Another severe penalty is the sense of guilt. One cannot escape self-condemnation and a loss of self-respect as a result of such sin.

KEEP YOURSELF PURE FOR MARRIAGE.

(Proverbs 5:15-20)

Drink waters out of thine own cistern, and running waters out of thine own well. Let thy fountain be blessed: and rejoice with the wife of thy youth.—Provverbs 5:15, 18

Purity is important for a successful marriage. True love for one's wife or husband depends upon virginity. If unfaithfulness has existed, there will never be the love there would have been, and this cementing power of love is lost. Many times it ends in a broken home, or at least in an unhappy home.

Many marriages end in divorce because of pre-marital experience. Neither partner can trust the other after they are married. This lack of confidence often leads to future unfaithfulness and finally divorce.

Illicit love never fully satisfies, either!

GOD WILL JUDGE SEXUAL SIN

(Proverbs 5:21-23)

For the ways of a man are before the eyes of the Lord, and he pondereth all his goings.—Proverbs 5:21

God sees all that we do. Furthermore, He also ponders our acts and the paths that we walk. Sin is never hidden from God, nor is it overlooked as being insignificant. Always remember—God is watching you!

We trap ourselves when we commit lustful acts. We enslave ourselves to our flesh, and we cease to be masters of self. We lose self control. Such sin leads eventually to an early death (verse 23).

Sound Business Principles

*My son, if thou be surety for thy friend . . . thou art
snared with the words of thy mouth.*—Proverbs 6:1, 2

Some years ago, a young minister began his ministry in a
small community in Missouri in a revival campaign. He was
entertained in the home of the president of the local bank.
The banker said to the young minister, "I want you to make
me a promise, and you are to keep it for life. I want you to
promise me that you will never, ever be surety for anyone.
Never sign anyone's note for a loan. I want you to make this
promise to me now, so that when people come to you to ask
you to go surety, you may honestly say, 'I cannot go
surety for you, because I have promised I never would, and
I must keep my promise.' It will give you an excuse to say
no. Will you promise?"

The young minister promised the president of the bank he
would never be anyone's surety. Since then, the president of
the bank has died, but the young minister has been faithful
to his promise. "That promise," he said, "has saved me from
the loss not only of much money; it has saved me from the
loss of many friends."

The best way to lose a friend is to be surety for him.
Friends soon become enemies when they owe you money.
The Bible admonishes, "Owe no man anything, but to love
him." (Romans 13:8).

A person can soon come to poverty and bankruptcy as a
result of being surety for a friend. Even if you love a person, you will not help him by going bankrupt with him!

Many things are to be considered before agreeing to be
surety for a person. First of all, will you be capable of paying
the loan should the borrower be unable to do so? If not,
it would be dishonest for you to be surety. Your signature

46

s evidence of your confidence in the security of the note
you sign.

Second, should a person borrow money for anything if he
s unable to produce collateral for the loan?

Third should you take the risk of signing a note to secure
he bank's loan when the bank makes all the profit? What
do you have to gain in taking the risk? If the bank cannot
ake the risk without your signature, then why should you?
A person who needs surety may be weak in character and
poor in business.

If you are willing to take the risk and be surety because
you love a person, or wish to help a person, then would it
not be better to give him the money, or make a personal
oan if you are capable of doing so?

Regardless, you should make sure that you will be able
o make good on the loan in case the borrower fails to pay.
You should consider carefully the consequences should you
pe forced to make good your signature.

The Bible is a practical guide to the Christian in every
phase of life, including business and economics. Most cer-
ainly, Christian ethics are involved in being surety on a
oan, and also in asking a person to go surety for you.

DO NOT BE LAZY

(Proverbs 6:4–11)

*Yet a little sleep, a little slumber, a little folding of
the hands to sleep: so shall thy poverty come as one that
travelleth, and thy want as an armed man.*—Proverbs
6:10–11

Some years ago, a Bible School student, who had an
average I.Q. was valedictorian of her class. Another student
with an I.Q. of a genius earned a much lower grade. The
genius studied very little and coasted through school. The
honor student burned midnight oil every night. She worked
hard, because her parents were sending her to school at great
sacrifice, and she considered that she owed it to them to take
full advantage of her education. Furthermore, as a Chris-
ian, she wished to gain all the knowledge she could, so
hat she could use her talents for the Lord to the fullest
xtent. Christian ethics entered into her studiousness.

Paul wrote to the Ephesians that a servant should be a
good servant "as unto Christ" (Ephesians 6:5–8). We will

be rewarded at the judgment seat of Christ on the basis of our faithfulness in business. A housewife will be rewarded for being industrious. Whatever we do, we should do it for the glory of Christ (Colossians 3:17, 23). Our life, whether it be in the home or in the shop or office, either glorifies Christ or else it reflects against Christ. Most certainly a minister, Sunday school teacher, church office worker, deacon, trustee or any other servant working directly for Christ should be diligent in labor. It is a sin to do the work of the Lord carelessly (Jeremiah 48:10).

Genius is actually labor. Success is in proportion to diligence in our task and labor expended. The have-nots envy the ones who have, but they too could have if they would study and work. Knowledge makes it possible to earn money but too many who are unwilling to make the sacrifice required to learn, and are unwilling to work hard and efficiently, want the fruits of labor without the labor.

Proverbs 6:4–11 gives us lessons from nature. Study these birds and animals and learn a lesson from them in success!

AVOID SHIFTY CHARACTERS

(Proverbs 6:12–19)

A naughty person, a wicked man, walketh with a froward mouth. He winketh with his eyes, he speaketh with his feet, he teacheth with his finger; Frowardness is in his heart, he deviseth mischief continually; he soweth discord.—Proverbs 6:12–14

The world is filled with lazy, shifty, rebellious people, who want money without work. Avoid them! Otherwise, you too will fail with them. Their lips lie; their eyes wink in deceit; their feet shuffle shiftlessly; their fingers make signs for they are always hiding their plans of deceit; their hearts are always scheming how to beat the honest man out of his money. They are traitors and mischief-makers. Avoid them else you will sin with them.

Shun Adultery

(Proverbs 7:1–23)

My son, keep my words, and lay up my commandments with thee. That they may keep thee from the strange woman . . . Let not thine heart decline to her ways, go not astray in her paths. For she hath cast down many wounded: yea, many strong men have been slain by her. Her house is the way to hell, going down to the chambers of death.—Proverbs 7:1, 5, 25–27

We are living in the days of "the new morality," which isn't at all new. It is the same old immorality which Proverbs warns against. Sin has not changed, and neither have its consequences. Morality is not a variable which reflects the viewpoint and custom of society. Righteousness is absolute. What is right is right, and what is wrong is wrong, regardless of what society approves or disapproves. Society's viewpoint depends on the spiritual condition of people, and conscience is an inner bell which reflects the moral training and spiritual condition of the human individual. But morality never changes. Only man's attitude toward morality changes. The consequences of sin remain the same.

Psychologists teach that one of the strongest drives in the human being is the sex drive. The sex urge may become uncontrollable without a spiritual restraint. Therefore it is of paramount importance that we recognize the dangers of the inner urge of sex which will bring either blessing or ruin. This sex drive must be controlled.

The temptress has the forces of nature working with her. Since the fall of man, sin and lust have been within the heart. The simple are the ones who fall into temptation (Proverbs 7:8), inviting sin. They toy with lust, and make a game of playing with fornication and adultery, thinking they can withdraw short of actual sin, but they are ignorant

49

and simple. It is difficult to resist temptation while experimenting with it. The best way to resist temptation is to avoid it.

A very necessary part of temptation is darkness (Proverbs 7:9). The human mind argues that if sin can be hidden, it will not be detected; then why not taste the forbidden fruit and see what it is like? But no sin is ever covered. God sees all and knows all. And be sure your sins will find you out. Sin in fornication is always a partnership, and no one can be sure that the partner in sin will remain confidential.

Improper dress is a part of the enticement for fornication and adultery (Proverbs 7:10). No decent woman will wear extremes of dress to entice men into sin. Improper dress is an invitation to sin, and those who dress immodestly will easily fall into sin. Temptation is the stepping stone to immorality.

There have always been dissolute persons who seek to tempt the moral person (Proverbs 7:12). This is but the stepping stone to sin itself. One slight step in the direction of sin often ends in gross immorality. Don't take that first, innocent step. Petting parties are only preparation for fornication. Beware! Once you start down this road, you may not be able to resist sin.

An offer to commit fornication will tempt only those who are willing (Proverbs 7:14–18). Your inner conviction will prevent you from sin, but if it is lacking, you will easily succumb to temptation.

The fornicator always convinces himself that his sin will be kept secret but such is not the case (Proverbs 7:19, 20). The person who yields to temptation is weak in character (Proverbs 7:21, 22). Be strong in the Lord (Ephesians 6:10–17).

PENALTY DESCRIBED

(Proverbs 6:25–35; 7:26, 27)

By means of a whorish woman a man is brought to a piece of bread . . . Can a man take fire in his bosom and his clothes not be burned? . . . Whoso committeth adultery with a woman lacketh understanding: he that doeth it destroyeth his own soul . . . a wound and dishonor shall he get.—Proverbs 6:26, 27, 32, 33

Before taking a leap, make sure where you will land! Never do anything without considering the consequences.

Fornication has many consequences. Millions are being deceived by the common acceptance of the "new morality," only to repent with tears later. What is the price of such sin?

Poverty is the first price (Proverbs 6:26). Visit Skid Row some day and talk to the men who are there and ask them how they arrived. They will tell you it was reached by the road adultery and drink. The two go together, and they lead to financial ruin.

Disease is another penalty. Syphilis is transmitted through fornication, and sooner or later, the person who commits this sin (and usually it is a repeated sin, once started) will soon become diseased. Venereal disease leads to insanity, heart disease, blindness, and many other serious health problems.

Other penalties of fornication are: *guilt* of conscience (6:29); *social rejection* (6:30, 31); *a lost soul* (6:32); *dishonor* (6:33); *vengeance* of a husband (6:34, 35); and *ruin* and *prison* (7:26); and *death* and *hell* (7:27).

PROTECTION THROUGH GOD'S WORD

(Proverbs 6:20-24; 7:1-4, 24)

For the commandment is a lamp; and the law is light; and reproofs of instruction are the ways of life: to keep thee from the evil woman, from the flattery of the tongue of the strange woman.—Proverbs 6:23, 24

The same Bible that has safely led your father and mother should be your guide (Proverbs 6:20, 21). David said, "Thy word have I hid in mine heart, that I might not sin against thee (Psalm 119:11). An ounce of prevention is worth more than a pound of cure. The Bible is a protection night and day (Proverbs 6:22). It is a light which removes the cloak for temptation. You should live by the Word, and obey God's Word. It will shield you from temptation and adultery (Proverbs 7:1-4, 24).

Christ, the Great Deliverer

WISDOM IN PROVERBS IS CHRIST

(Proverbs 8:22 31)

*The Lord possessed me in the beginning of his way,
before his works, of old. I was set up from everlasting,
from the beginning, or ever the earth was. When there
were no depths, I was brought forth . . . I was by him,
as one brought up with him: I was daily his delight . . .
Whoso findeth me findeth life . . . they that hate me
love death.*—Proverbs 8:22–24, 30, 35, 36

When Pilate asked Jesus who he was, Jesus replied, "I
am truth." Colossians 2:3 says of Christ Jesus, "In whom are
hid all the treasures of wisdom and knowledge." The wisdom of God is beyond measure. The mind that conceived
creation and planned its mathematical forces that hold the
universe in orbit is beyond human conception. Christ is the
sum total of all wisdom. He is the God of the atom, who
planned it and holds it together. He planned the basic ele-
ments of creation and gave each one its mathematical value
and valence, its color which identifies it, and its electrical value peculiar to its singular property. Think for a moment of
the historic knowledge, the scientific knowledge of the God
of all time and creation. Christ is the "I AM" who appeared
to Moses in Exodus 3:14, the eternally existent One, the all-
knowing One.

Proverbs 8:22 tells us that Christ is the eternally existent
God. He always was, always is, and always will be (John 1:1;
Proverbs 8:22–31). Christ is the God of creation. Proverbs
8:25–29 informs us that Christ was living when the creation
was brought into being. John 1:4 and Colossians 1:16 tell
us that all things were made by Christ. Hebrews 1:10, quot-
ing the Psalmist, says, "Thou Lord in the beginning hast
laid the foundations of the earth; and the heavens are the

52

works of thine hands." Truly Christ is the one called "Wisdom" in Proverbs 8:22–31.

Proverbs 8:30 says, "I was with him, as one brought up with him: and I was daily his delight, rejoicing always before him." The original text of John 1:1 states similarly, "In the beginning was the Logos (incarnate wisdom), and the Logos was face to face in fellowship with God, and God was the Logos!" Plato had coined the usage of the name Logos for the one who would redeem the world, and the word Logos means wisdom. John answers and corrects the fallacy of Plato who said the Logos would be like God, but not God. John states clearly the Logos was God.

TO FIND CHRIST IS TO FIND ETERNAL LIFE

(Proverbs 8:32–36)

Whoso findeth me findeth life, and shall obtain favour of the Lord. But he that sinneth against me wrongeth his own soul: all they that hate me love death.—Proverbs 8:35, 36

To find Christ and to know Him is to have eternal life. Jesus said, "This is eternal life, that they might know thee the only true God, and Jesus Christ, whom thou hast sent" (John 17:3). Paul gave up all things that he might know Christ (Philippians 3:7–9). Salvation is not attained by a way of thinking, nor by a way of living, but through a person, the Saviour, the Lord Jesus Christ. You must *know* Him. You must trust Him, believe in Him, submit yourself to Him, rely on Him.

So it is that Proverbs 8:32 says we are to keep His ways. We are also to have daily communion and fellowship with the person of Christ (Proverbs 8:34).

Salvation comes, however, when we find Him (Proverbs 8:35). It was Andrew who first found the Lord, and immediately he sought out his brother, Simon, and said, "We have found the Messias, which is, being interpreted, the Christ" (John 1:41). Have you made this great discovery? Have you found the Christ, the Saviour of the World? Do you know Him? Is He your Saviour? Do you know Him, not as an historical character, but as a personal Saviour, and as your Lord?

To reject Christ is to sin against Him. This is the unpardonable sin referred to in Mark 3:28–30. To reject Christ is to sin against you own soul (Proverbs 8:36). To hate and reject Christ is to love and choose death, eternal death! (Proverbs 8:36).

CHRIST CALLS US TO A RIGHTEOUS LIFE

(Proverbs 8:1–21)

All the words of my mouth are in righteousness; there is nothing froward or perverse in them. The fear of the Lord is to hate evil: pride, and arrogancy, and the evil way . . . I lead in the way of righteousness, in the midst of the paths of judgment.—Proverbs 8:8, 13, 20

We are saved by faith in a living person, Jesus Christ. Christ is the Saviour, and not we ourselves. Therefore, nothing we do can save us, nor help to save us. We are saved by grace, through faith (Ephesians 2:8–10). We are saved without the deeds of the law (Romans 3:20–28). But we are saved unto good works (Ephesians 2:10). Good works cannot save us, but if our faith is real, it will produce good works (James 2:17, 18). Christ is righteous, and if He dwells within our hearts, He will make us righteous.

Proverbs 8:1–21 dwells upon this new life, the life of righteousness which Christ imparts when we are saved by faith. Christ cries to us, calling us to a righteous life (Proverbs 8:1–7).

Righteousness begins within the heart, but it expresses itself through the lips. Jesus said it was not what men take into the body through the lips which stained them, but that which came from the evil heart through the lips that made them guilty. Emphasis is laid upon purity of our lips in Proverbs 8:7–9.

To know Christ, and to live righteously is of more value than silver or gold (Proverbs 8:10, 11). The song, "I'd Rather Have Jesus," is but a sermon on these verses.

If the heart is right with God, it will love the Lord and righteousness, but it will hate sin. Our very attitude will be changed. Old things will pass away, and all things will become new. The Christian *hates* evil. He does more than give it up. Evil is summed up as pride, arrogancy, the evil way of living and walking, the froward (rebellious and contrary) mouth.

The Christian finds counsel for righteous living from the Lord (Proverbs 8:14). Christ is his strength (Proverbs 8:14; Philippians 4:13).

The Christian life is a successful life, for the Lord gives

his children wisdom, and He blesses them (Proverbs 8:15–21). Christ Jesus said, "Seek ye first the kingdom of God, and His righteousness, and *all these things shall be added unto you* (Matthew 6:33).

Life's Greatest Choice

(Proverbs 9:1–12)

Wisdom hath builded her house, she hath hewn out her seven pillars . . . Come, eat of my bread, and drink of the wine which I have mingled. Forsake the foolish and live; and go in the way of understanding.—Proverbs 9:1, 5, 6

The figures of speech in this chapter are easily understood. Wisdom is the Lord Jesus Christ as we learned in the last chapter. The palace referred to undoubtedly is the church on earth, but more than that, it is the palace in heaven above. Christ has gone to prepare a place for us. He is building a mansion in glory for us. It is said of Abraham, "He looked for (waited for) a city which hath foundations, whose builder and maker is God" (Hebrews 11:10). The psalmist refers to this heavenly palace in Psalm 48:3, 12–14.

A great feast has been prepared for all, and the invitation has gone forth throughout the earth, calling and inviting all who will, to come and attend the feast. Great preparation has been made. The fatted calf has been killed, and the wine has been prepared. The wine symbolizes the blood of Christ, and the slain animal symbolizes Christ, the Lamb of God, that taketh away the sin of the world.

Christ gave a similar parable in Luke 14:16–24. Guests were invited to a great supper, but they immediately began to make excuses and refused to attend. The master of the house was angry and commanded his servants to go into the highways and byways, to invite the poor, the lame, and the blind to attend. He swore that none who had refused his invitation would ever taste of his supper. Similarly, in Proverbs 9:2, great preparation has been made for the heavenly banquet awaiting those who will accept the call and invitation which God has extended to all who will attend. Those who refuse will suffer the consequences.

Salvation is offered to all men. The preparation for heaven's great supper required the death of Jesus Christ on the cross, and the spilling of His blood for our redemption. Salvation was bought at a mighty cost. Beware if you ignore or refuse God's invitation after He has paid such a high price.

Christ cries from every corner of the world inviting sinners to be saved, calling through His servants, His missionaries, His ministers of the gospel. He also warns those who will refuse, that judgment awaits lost sinners, without Christ Jesus as Saviour.

The man without Christ has been deceived, and is therefore referred to as being simple. He is promised enlightenment and understanding of spiritual things if he will come (Proverbs 9:4).

Christ offers food for the soul of the sinner if he will come and receive Christ (Proverbs 9:5). Christ dwells in us and is our spiritual strength. Compare John 6:53-58.

But to be a Christian, there is a price to be paid (Proverbs 9:6). We must at the same time forsake sin and sinful companionship if we are to live. We are to walk in the way of understanding, or righteousness.

We may also expect to be rejected by our former companions of sin. They will mock us and scorn us (Proverbs 9:8). We cannot please Christ and sinners at the same time; we must choose between them. Someone asks, "Then must I give up my old friends?" Our answer is, "No! They will give you up!"

The Christian grows in wisdom and the knowledge of the Lord. From the moment he is saved he grows and progresses.

To educate a criminal is to make a better criminal. But to educate a good man, a Christian, is to make him more useful for both God and man. Man requires salvation before education, for education cannot change the man, but Christ does. Once a man is transformed through the redemptive powers of Christ, education will increase his value (Proverbs 9:9).

The world thinks that a Christian is peculiar or even mad (Acts 26:24), but the truth is that wisdom begins with the fear, reverence, and worship of the Lord (Proverbs 9:10). Furthermore, life becomes more worthwhile when we know Christ (Proverbs 9:11). The days will grow more profitable and the years more fruitful.

To have Christ is to have wisdom, for all wisdom is hid in Christ Jesus. And to have Him is to have the reward of all knowledge and truth within you. What a privilege it is to be a Christian (Proverbs 9:12).

FOLLY ALSO CALLS YOU

(Proverbs 9:13–18)

A foolish woman is clamorous: she is simple, and knoweth nothing. For she sitteth at the door of her house . . . to call passengers who go right on their ways: Whoso is simple, let him turn in hither . . . He knoweth not that the dead are there: and that her guests are in the depths of hell.—Proverbs 9:13–16, 18

The foolish woman in verse 13 is a prostitute. She represents all sin calling us away from God, from truth, and from salvation. She is clamorous, making much noise. The world is not at all adverse to parading its temptation. She is very open in parading her wares of sin. On every hand she is beckoning the sinner away from God.

Temptation and the enticement of sin is everywhere—on the high places of the city, and at every open door (Proverbs 9:14)! She is very busy calling and encouraging men to depart from God (Proverbs 9:15). Oh that Christians were as faithful and bold in inviting men to Christ as sinners are unashamed to call people into sin.

There are many simple ones who stumble before the onslaughts of sin and wickedness. They choose sin and eternal hell when they refuse Christ and salvation. Those who are wise will not make this foolish mistake (Proverbs 9:16–18). The sinner thinks only of the pleasant fruits of sin which are but for a moment; he overlooks the fact that the end of the sinner's life is death and hell.

Three Rewards for Righteousness

You Will Not Famish

(Proverbs 10:3)

The Lord will not suffer the soul of the righteous to famish: but he casteth away the substance of the wicked.
—Proverbs 10:3

Beginning with Chapter 10, many proverbs are in contrast, revealing the advantage of the Christian life over the wicked life. In our study today, we wish to use the lot of the wicked only as a background to make the beauty of the righteous life stand forth as supreme. We will emphasize the beauty of the righteous life and behold its advantages.

The use of the word "soul" in our text would indicate that this promise that the righteous will not famish has reference to the spiritual side of man rather than the physical. It is true that God will supply our every temporal need. David said, "I have been young, and now am old; yet have I not seen the righteous forsaken, nor his seed begging bread" (Psalm 37:25). God is concerned about our physical welfare. He does cause the food to grow, and billions of animals as well as billions of people feed at His table daily. Where there is want, it is due to man's sin and wickedness, not due to God's failure to make the seed to grow into fruition and food.

Nevertheless the spiritual food of man is more important than the temporal food of man. Jesus said, "Man shall not live by bread alone, but by every word that proceedeth out of God" (Matthew 4:4). The unrighteous are hungry, not so much for food as for soul satisfaction, and they do not find it. The righteous are satisfied. They feed at God's table, and their souls are made fat.

America is competing with Communist countries on a mere temporal basis, but the one food we have which they lack is spiritual food. This is the food that satisfies the soul of man. This is the food mankind yearns for and seeks. Let us challenge the atheist nations on the basis that we offer food for the soul.

The righteous soul shall not famish for three reasons. First, as the psalmist said, "The Lord is my shepherd, I shall not want" (Psalm 23:1). As a shepherd cares for his sheep, guiding them into green pastures and beside the still waters, so the Lord leads us into quiet places and gives us refreshing, spiritual, sparkling waters of life. Our shepherd, the Lord Jesus Christ, is ever with us, so how could we possibly want for anything? He is able to do exceeding abundantly above all we will ever ask or even think.

Second, our souls shall not famish because Jesus never fails. Psalm 37 is a favorite psalm of all Christians. Here we are promised, "Trust in the Lord, and do good; so shalt thou dwell in the land, and *verily thou shalt be fed.*" There is nothing our Lord cannot do, and there is nothing He will not do for us if it is for our good, for He loves us. If He has given His life for us, will He not freely give us all things? (Roman 8:32; Isaiah 43:3, 4).

Third, we shall never want, because the Lord is an inexhaustible storehouse. John 1:16 has been translated, "And from the bounties of his storehouse have we all received one spiritual blessing heaped upon another spiritual blessing." Luke 6:38 promises both spiritual and temporal blessings. Believers have been claiming Philippians 4:19 for generations, and this promise has never been exhausted. It has not been denied once. God fulfills His pledge always.

YOUR MEMORY WILL BE BLESSED

The memory of the just is blessed: but the name of the wicked shall rot.—Proverbs 10–7

Millions come and go, and are soon forgotten. Some live forever in the memory of mankind. They may not be rich nor famous, and yet they live on. Dorcas is an example of such a person. She was but a seamstress who dedicated her needle to the Lord and to the poor, and she will never be forgotten!

There are three reasons the name of the righteous will never be forgotten: First, famous deeds make famous men! Mary of Bethany was a nobody until she anointed the Lord

Jesus Christ with the expensive ointment (Matthew 26:6–13). Jesus said her name would never be forgotten, and to this day, it is remembered and sermons are preached about her devotion and sacrifice in praise. Her deed and worship made her famous. So she still lives on.

Second, God never forgets our good deeds, and He will reward those who are stedfast and faithful. This is an encouragement to good works and righteousness. See I Corinthians 15:58.

Third, our good deeds never die; they live on forever. God told Cornelius, "Thy prayers and thine alms are come up for a memorial before God" (Acts 10:4). Even when we reach heaven, our alms will still live as an everlasting memorial!

YOU WILL WALK SURELY

He that walketh uprightly walketh surely: but he that perverteth his ways shall be known.—Proverbs 10:9

The psalmist said in Psalm 73:18 that the wicked walked in slippery places. But it is said of the righteous, that his foot shall not be moved. Psalm 40:2 is a testimony of the righteous that when he is saved, "He brought me out of an horrible pit, out of the miry clay, and *set my feet upon a rock, and established my goings.*"

The sinner is apt to slip at any time, for he walks near temptation, but the Christian stands upon the Rock, Christ Jesus.

Second, "the steps of the righteous man are ordered of the Lord" (Psalm 37:23). God has promised that He will guide us with His eye (Psalm 32:8). God has also promised to guide us with His counsel (Psalm 73:24). Christ promised us in John 14:16 that He would send to us the Holy Spirit as our "paraclete." The word paraclete is a Greek word, combining two words: "to walk," and "along side of." The Holy Spirit not only guides us in the way, He also walks with us as our guide and companion.

Third, the righteous walk on God's highways of holiness (Isaiah 35:8–10). Read and study this passage carefully. In the book of Ephesians, the walk of the Christian is described: (1) The Christian walks worthy of his vocation or calling (Ephesians 4:1). (2) The Christian walks not as pagans walk (Ephesians 4:17). (3) The Christian walks in love (Ephesians 5:2). (4) The Christian walks as "children of light" (Ephesians 5:8). (5) The Christian walks circumspectly (Ephesians 5:15). Truly, the Christian walk is a surefooted walk!

Three Divine Blessings

HE MAKETH RICH

The blessing of the Lord, it maketh rich, and he addeth no sorrow with it.—Proverbs 10:22

There are three things concerning the Lord which we should consider in Proverbs, Chapter 10: (1) The *blessing* of the Lord (verse 22); (2) The *fear* of the Lord (verse 27); (3) The *way* of the Lord (verse 29). Then there are three results: He "maketh rich," "prolongeth days," and "is strength."

First, we learn the secret of riches. Riches are not necessarily a matter of astuteness, or cleverness, but rather a blessing from the Lord. In II Kings 5:1 we read that Naaman was a great man, because by him the Lord had given victory unto the armies of Syria. There are no self-made men, only God-made men. Naaman was not a worshipper of Jehovah, but God had seen fit to bless him, knowing what he would be later.

Job said, "The Lord hath given, and the Lord hath taken away, blessed be the name of the Lord." Job was reduced from riches to ashes and poverty, but in the end the Lord blessed him again, and gave him twice the wealth he had enjoyed before.

Joseph was sold as a slave, but he was promoted by God until he became a ruler of Egypt. God crowned him through the pathway of the dungeon and prison.

Whom God will, He promotes and exalts. And whom God will, He reduces to nothingness. Our very life is in His hands. He can bless if He so chooses.

And God will be no man's debtor. He has promised to bless those who are liberal and who give. See Luke 6:38. R. G. LeTourneau, the well-known industrialist often said, "Giving to God is like playing a game of 'give-away.' The more you give, the more you get, and you can't beat God a giving!"

Whom does God bless? "The liberal soul shall be made fat." Those who are tight and selfish are never blessed.

God will not bless those who disobey Him. Nor will He bless the backslider, or the person out of fellowship with Him. God will not bless those who use their influence for sin and Satan. He will not bless those who do not walk uprightly.

God can bless you, or He can take away from you.

A multimillionaire in Cleveland, Ohio, said, "Once I was worth more than three million dollars, but I forgot the Lord and lived carelessly, neglecting my worship and daily devotions. God took all of my wealth from me and reduced me to ashes and want. Then I prayed and promised to honor Him with my tithes and with my life. God began to bless me again. Today, I have already made my second million and am making even more."

What are the riches God gives to men? Does He reward us only with silver and gold? Money cannot make you happy nor can it make life worth living. God gives riches far more important than silver and gold. He does bless with money, but the riches most to be sought after are the riches of children, a home, happiness, and health. Character is our greatest human prize which He gives. Friends and fellowship with other Christians is a treasure of great value. Wealthy is the man who has these treasures.

Your church is your greatest treasure on earth. What a blessing to be able to go to the house of the Lord, to worship God, to sing praises to His name, and to know other Christians. To learn of His Word and to enter into His tabernacle is life's greatest blessing.

God's presence with you daily is more important than houses and lands, stocks and bonds, and money in the bank.

Knowledge is another great treasure. The more you know the more avenues of interest are opened to you in life. Divine knowledge is the most important knowledge of all.

The Bible is a divine revelation of God, and it is eternal truth. Its promises are sure and valuable. Is there any earthly treasure to compare with this?

The life of the Christian is truly made rich!

HE PROLONGETH DAYS

*The fear of the Lord prolongeth days: but the years of
the wicked shall be shortened.*—Proverbs 10:27

"To prolong days" is to stretch out the days, and to get
the most out of life. The Christian lives more while he lives
than does the sinner. The Christian does not shorten his
days with sin, and he enjoys each day to the fullest extent.
He enjoys living. The sinner often despairs of life, and con-
cludes it is not worth living. He may even seek to destroy his
own life. He has nothing for which to live; his life is often
a drudgery and a disappointment. What a contrast was the
testimony of Paul who said, "For me to live is Christ" (Philippians 1:21). Paul had something to live for, and therefore a goal to strive toward.

The sinner shortens his days through sin. A doctor who
specializes in cancer research said, "For every cigarette you
smoke, you may deduct fourteen and one-half minutes from
your life." So it is with sin. Each act of sin will shorten your
life, and also destroy the joy of living.

The Christian has peace both in mind and heart, for his
conscience is free from guilt. Happiness depends on joy
within the heart and not upon environment. The Christian's
heart is right with God. Therefore his days are lengthened.

HE GIVETH STRENGTH

*The way of the Lord is strength to the upright: but de-
struction shall be to the workers of iniquity.*—Proverbs
10:29

Angels strengthened Elijah after his conflict with the
prophets of Baal and Jezebel. The angels ministered to
Christ after the forty days of temptation in the wilderness.
And His angels will strengthen you after the heat of the bat-
tles of life. The Psalmist expressed this beautifully: "He
anointeth my head with oil" (Psalm 23:5).

God has promosed, "As thy days, so shall thy strength
be" (Deuteronomy 33:25). No matter what the test, He
will supply the need and strength to meet that test.

God gives strength to meet the enemy, Satan (Ephesians
6:10–17). He gives strength to meet temptation and to resist it (Romans 7:24–8:2). Read Proverbs 24:10.

Three Kindred Evils

HATRED STIRRETH STRIFE

Hatred stirreth up strifes: but love covereth all sins.
—Proverbs 10:12

One of the most common sins among Christians is hatred.
Hate smolders within their hearts and becomes a source of
great trouble not only to the person who is hated; but it also
poisons the hearts and souls of those who hate. Hate may
disrupt an entire church or community. Hate breeds murder and wars. That is why Jesus warned that whosoever calls
his brother a fool is in danger of hell fire (Matthew 5:21,
22). Few murders are committed in cold blood, nor with
forethought and premeditation. Murder happens when hate
explodes into uncontrollable emotion. Hate is a sin to be
feared and shunned. We should daily cleanse our hearts of
all malice and hate.

As we consider this horrible, and yet common sin, let us
evaluate it from our own personal standpoint. What does hate
do to me? First, it can cause ill health and also rob me of
peace of mind. Hate pours out a poison into the blood
stream. It causes glandular activity to perform out of balance. It drains and saps the vitality. It can cause serious
illness which will eventually bring me to an early grave.

Second, hate will rob me of success in business. Successful
executives and leaders of business and politics are men who
are pleasant. They love people. They are kind, overlooking
faults, and they never carry grudges. An employer will not
knowingly hire a person who harbors hate and carries grudges,
for such a person stirs up strife among other employees,
hindering production. Therefore the man who hates may find
it difficult to find employment, and certainly, he will be the
first one to be laid off during a slack season.

Third, hate destroys friendships. People avoid close friendships with persons whose souls are bitter with hate. The
hate-filled person is a lonely person. Why should anyone seek

fellowship with such a person? Who would want to be around a hate-filled person? He is to be avoided!

Fourth, hate destroys your own personal happiness and robs you of the joy of living. What joy is there in hating?

Now for a moment, let us consider what hate does to the person who is hated. Obviously, it causes much misery and heartache. A Christian is always careful to make others happy, not miserable. The Golden Rule controls his every act.

Hate will cause others to retaliate. Hate and you will be hated. Hate engenders strife and a quarrel. People who hate always seek converts to champion their cause. A small match of hate can ignite a world war!

Hate robs the Christian of his testimony. Who can believe in Christianity when its followers hate one another? Jesus said men would know that we are his disciples because we love one another, not hate one another. Love is the very heart and essence of Christianity. Hate was the force that Satan used in the beginning. It led Cain to murder Abel. The philosopher, Neitzsche, taught that hate is a more powerful force than love, and therefore it should be relied upon rather than love. He believed that hate would conquer the world. But love will win, not hate. To love is divine; to hate is Satanic. To love is positive goodness; to hate is a negative vacuum. Love is good; hate is evil. Good will eventually conquer evil, for God is good, and God is love.

Hate stirs up strife and trouble. Love generates peace (James 3:18).

A FALSE BALANCE IS AN ABOMINATION

A false balance is abomination to the Lord: but a just weight is his delight.—Proverbs 11:1

If a false balance is an abomination unto the Lord, what does He think of the person who puts large tomatoes on the top of the basket, and small ones underneath? And what does God think of the person who brings spoiled canned goods to the church Harvest Home Service and keeps the best for himself?

A false balance is a revelation of what a person is. The man who will be false in measuring or weighing that which he sells is mean, miserly, selfish, and self-centered. He is dishonest, and he will cheat in every way possible if he thinks he can succeed in his deception. He is not to be trusted. He is a liar at heart, and a thief.

A false weight makes a person feel mean. He cannot respect himself, and neither can anyone else. A cheat is a very small person.

No one who uses a false weight in any respect has a good influence on others. Sinners will not hear his testimony. He cannot be a soul winner. He cannot witness to the saving power of Christ, for his own heart needs changing.

A false witness is a deceiver in the sight of God. And God sees through his perfidy. God will not bless him, nor reward him either here or hereafter. Think twice before you cheat anyone! You are only cheating yourself. The person who cheats once only loses future business, for no intelligent person will ever do business with him again.

A TALEBEARER REVEALETH SECRETS

(Proverbs 11:13; 18:8; 20:19)

A talebearer revealeth secrets: but he that is a faithful spirit concealeth the matter.—Proverbs 11:13

"A dog that will bring a bone will carry a bone." Beware of the person who brings confidential information to you. He is not to be trusted. Avoid him, and save yourself trouble (Proverbs 20:19).

It is kind to hide some things, even if they are true (Proverbs 11:13). Because a tale is true does not give you license to tell it. Ask yourself, "Is it kind to tell it? Will it help the person involved in the story? Would I want anyone to tell such a story about me?" Do unto others as you would have them do unto you.

The tongue is a very dangerous weapon (Proverbs 18:8). With it you can cruelly kill a person with slow death, by piercing his heart with trouble.

The Blessedness of Giving

THE LAW OF SOWING AND REAPING

(Galatians 6:7–9; II Corinthians 9:6)

There is that scattereth, and yet increaseth; and there is that withholdeth more than is meet, but it tendeth to poverty.—Proverbs 11:24

Some people have so little because they give so little. The soul of the penurious person is never made fat. The stingy are never blessed.

A businessman said, "I used to say, I can't afford to tithe my income and give it to God, but now I have learned that I cannot afford not to tithe. When I started tithing, my money went farther, and I had less expenses for repairs, hospitals, and accidents."

A minister in Ohio said, "All of my members tithe!"

The person to whom he said it was amazed. "How did you ever succeed in getting all of your members to tithe?" he asked dubiously.

"I didn't," was the reply. "God did."

"How's that?"

"They either pay their tithes willingly to God, or else God collects it from them through sickness, failure, or accident."

One man refused to tithe. He discovered to his amazement at the end of the year that he had paid out in bills for sickness and accident exactly the amount equal to his tithe!

Any farmer knows that if he plants only a bushel of wheat, he will not reap as much wheat as he would have reaped if he had planted one hundred bushels. This is only logical and obvious. Is it not just as obvious that this principle of sowing and reaping applies in every phase of our life? The person who does evil will reap evil in an equal proportion.

69

If he sows in giving to the work of preaching the gospel, he will reap in multitudinous blessings and income in business. God can and does bless the faithful ones.

Notice, however, that we always reap much more than we sow. A farmer who plants a bushel of wheat expects to reap many more bushels than he sows. It is God who puts life into the seed and makes it grow. It is God who bathes it with rain and sunshine. God multiplies it. And God will multiply whatever you may give to Him.

A farmer in Michigan started giving one-tenth of all his wheat to God, and replanted it. In a few years he was compelled to discontinue, for there would not have been enough soil on earth to continue the experiment.

A vase of seed was found in one of the tombs of an Egyptian Pharaoh. A scientist estimated that if these few seeds had been planted and replanted during the thousands of years that had passed since the seed was hidden in the tomb, the earth would long since been overrun with wheat. This same law is operative when you give to God. The little you give, and the little you do for God will multiply until the entire earth may be changed through your gifts.

If you had invested ten thousand dollars in mutual funds and stocks in 1945 and allowed the dividends to be reinvested, today you would be worth more than one hundred and thirty thousand dollars! What if you had given that same ten thousand dollars to preach Christ? What would the results be today? The same law of sowing and reaping applies, and the world might have changed its course.

"Be not weary in well doing, for in due season you shall reap if you faint not." This promise is not provisional. God didn't say you *might* reap; He said you *shall* reap.

You have only one life. Invest it well for God and you will reap an eternal reward. Make your life count. Make it worthwhile. Be careful in investing your time, your talents, and your income for the glory of Christ.

GOD'S REWARD

(Malachi 3:10; II Corinthians 9:8–11)

The liberal shoul shall be made fat.—Proverbs 11:25

Do you believe that God is able to bless you and to give you success? Do you believe that He is able to withhold blessing from you? He most assuredly is. He is the one who can give health. He can open doors of opportunity. He can lead you into paths of abundance or into the desert place.

Did you ever consider why God does not bless you in the same way He blesses others? He is sovereign, and it is important to be yielded to Him and to accept His will.

A young man asked a minister, "Why doesn't God bless me with millions of dollars as He did LeTourneau?"

The minister replied, "Be honest. Would you have been faithful in giving to God's work as LeTourneau was? Tell the truth."

After a moment of heart searching, the young man replied, "I guess not."

"That is why God does not bless you as he did LeTourneau," the minister said.

God has challenged every one of us to tithe. He will be no man's debtor. He has promised that if we tithe, He will bless us beyond our capacity to receive. God cannot lie. He said, "Prove me!" He is challenging you to prove Him, to put Him to the test. He is waiting for you to do so. Why don't you?

Jacob proved God by making a covenant to tithe in Genesis 28:22. God accepted Jacob's challenge and began to bless him so much that his father-in-law became very jealous. No matter what bargain Laban made with Jacob, Jacob was the winner. And Jacob remembered to give God the credit. God can and does bless whom He will.

MAN'S REWARD

(Luke 6:38; II Corinthians 9:12–14)

He that watereth shall be watered also himself.—Proverbs 11:25

The liberal soul shall be made fat. People love generous people. They give to them, because they love them. A miser has no friends, but the liberal soul has many friends, and they turn their business his way.

A man who sold more life insurance than any other salesman that year was asked by a friend, "How did you do it?"

"I didn't," the salesman replied. "I never asked one single person to buy one single insurance policy. I made friends with wealthy people, and they sent for me and bought their insurance through me."

Better yet, when you give the gospel to others, they in turn will glorify Christ. Can you ask for a better reward?

Winning Souls

THE ART OF SOUL WINNING

The fruit of righteousness is a tree of life; and he that winneth souls is wise.—Proverbs 11:30

Soul winning is an art. Not everyone is successful in winning men to Christ. If we are to succeed, we must carefully study the methods of soul winning which Scriptures reveal. Let us study the Word and see what soul winning really is.

First, soul winning is witnessing (Acts 1:8). God did not ask angels to win souls; this privilege is reserved solely to men, because only one who has experienced the saving and redemptive power of Christ can witness to the lost. To encourage others to believe, we must show them an example of salvation. We must become demonstrators. Our life is a witness for or against Christ. Our words are a witness to the power of Christ. We do not tell people what our views of theology are to win them to Christ. We merely tell them what God has done for us and what He can do for them. Any saved person can witness, but not all could argue theology. You may not be capable of defending the faith, but you can reveal the power of God in your own life.

Soul winning is, second, *seeking* the lost. Read carefully the entire chapter of Luke 15. Here we have three illustrations of seeking the lost. We are to go after them and bring them back to the fold. We are to seek until we find.

Third, soul winning is *sharing* Christ with our own loved ones and friends. It was just natural for Andrew to seek out his brother and share the Messiah with him. We dare not hoard the gospel and hide it. We owe it to both Christ who died for lost sinners, and to our friends and loved ones, to share salvation.

Fourth, soul winning is *explaining* to a sinner his need of salvation, and then *to show* him the way of salvation. Jesus explained to Nicodemus how one is born again, and

He told him that he must be born again. He explained that salvation is a spiritual birth, accomplished by God, not man. It is by faith, not works. Jesus explained to the woman at the well in John 4 that salvation was a gift which must be accepted by simple faith. He illustrated the truth and made it simple by using water as an illustration. A soul winner must make clear and plain what salvation is, and how it is attained.

Fifth, salvation is *preaching* (Romans 10:14, 15). We must sow the seed of truth far and wide. We must show and forewarn the lost what the Word of God has to say concerning sin, eternal punishment, the lost condition of all sinners, and the judgment to come. We must show them the precious promises of God which give assurance of forgiveness of sins and eternal life.

Sixth, soul winning is *reasoning* with sinners (Isaiah 1: 18). The truths of God's Word are reasonable, and it is sound reasoning that must bring men to a consciousness that they are sinners and eternally lost. It is reasoning that brings them to decision.

Seventh, soul winning is *fishing* for men (Matthew 4:19). Fishing requires skill. The soul winner must know how to attract the sinner with good bait. He must hook the sinner with barbs within his conscience. He must net the sinner into the control of God. He must use every method known to man to catch the sinner in the net of God's truth.

THE FRUIT OF SOUL WINNING

The fruit of the righteous is a tree of life.—Proverbs 11:30

Winning souls is to be likened to planting a fruit tree. It grows and bears fruit in abundance in the future.

We do not expect to pick fruit the day we plant a tree. We wait years for the fruit to come. So it is with soul winning. How much fruit awaits you? Some of this fruit is picked here on earth, as we rejoice in the souls who have found the Lord, as we see them grow in the faith. Most of the fruit will be hereafter, however, in heaven.

Paul said that the souls he had won to Christ in Thessalonica were his crown of rejoicing (I Thessalonians 2:19, 20). Will your heart rejoice when you reach heaven, when souls who were saved through your efforts will come to you and thank you for having shown them the way to escape 'eternal death and how to go to heaven. What greater reward could you wish?

Jesus spoke of souls as a harvest field where the fruit was ripe and ready to be picked. He sent us forth to reap, and promised us that we would rejoice in the harvest of souls when we reach heaven (John 4:35–38).

Psalm 126:5, 6 gives us assurance that if we sow seed and water it with tears of prayer, we will harvest a crop of souls, and we will come rejoicing.

James 5:20 assures us of the joy of saving a soul from death, and covering a multitude of sins.

Daniel 12:3 promises that we will shine as the stars in the firmament forever if we win souls to Christ.

Billy Sunday won more than six million souls to Christ. What a crown he will wear! How many souls have you won? Jesus urged us to lay up treasures in heaven, and not on earth. How much treasure of souls have you stored in glory?

THE WISDOM OF SOUL WINNING

He that winneth souls is wise.—Proverbs 11:30

It not only is wise to win souls to Christ; it also requires much wisdom to win lost souls.

The first step in winning a soul is to have a hook. A button which invites a question will open the conversation leading up to witnessing. We call such a gimmick a hook. A wise man tactfully introduces salvation to a sinner.

Finding common ground of understanding is wise. Jesus used water as a common basis of understanding and interest when he talked to the woman at the well. He used water as a common ground to begin a conversation.

A compliment is better than a criticism in winning lost souls. We must win people; we cannot force them into salvation. We love them to God. We sow the seed of God's Word, and then water it with prayer. Then we must wait for the results.

The Poor Rich Man

THE RICH MAN WHO IS POOR

There is that maketh himself rich, yet hath nothing.
—Proverbs 13:7

Years ago, we dined with one of the wealthiest men in America. He dwelled in a mansion with many servants. His home overlooked the lake, and it was in the most elite section of the city. He lived in luxury every day, and he lacked nothing. The carpeting on the floor was an inch thick, and the walls were hung with individually-lighted oil paintings valued at millions of dollars. The meal was served on golden china, and the dinnerware was gold. But he could not eat! He had no health. His servants were quarreling, and the halls were cold because they lacked love and the laughter of children. I pitied this poor rich man!

Soon after, we visited a very poor man, who lived in a log cabin in the pine woods of Georgia. He was strumming his guitar and singing, while his wife was cooking a simple meal of corned beef and cabbage. There was no lawn surrounding his house—only white sand. There were no carpets in his house, and no glass windows. The furniture was simple and sparse; the house was almost empty. The only art to decorate the walls was a few calendar pictures which were unframed. The two rockers and two wooden chairs in the single room of the cabin needed varnish, but they were fairly comfortable. Yet, this man and his wife were immensely happy.

We asked ourselves, "What makes the difference?"

One thing was obvious: materialism cannot make a person happy. Wealth cannot buy happiness. Happiness is bred within the heart, and is not the result of environment. Happiness is a state of the mind and heart.

Wealth cannot buy friends. America is discovering this. The loneliest people on earth are often the wealthiest.

So neither can money buy salvation. Heaven is not for

sale. Jesus told of a certain rich man who fared sumptuously every day, and a poor beggar, Lazarus, lay at his gate, full of sores, begging for the crumbs that fell from the rich man's table. Both men died. In hell the rich man lifted up his eyes and saw Lazarus far off in Abraham's bosom. Earth circumstances did not determine eternal destiny. Riches did not send the rich man to hell, and poverty did not buy heaven for Lazarus. Salvation is a gift; so is heaven. (See Ephesians 2:8–10), I Peter 1:18; Luke 16:19–31; John 4:10).

Dr. R. E. Neighbour was preaching in Budapest, Hungary, when a man arose and held up a large roll of bills. "This is my god, preacher," he cried.

"Don't you feel sorry for this man?" Dr. Neighbour asked the audience. "His god cannot buy him health, life, happiness, nor peace. It cannot give him a new heart, nor can it take him to heaven. It cannot buy him a resurrection body, nor hope for life hereafter. When he dies he will lose his god, unless someone should steal it from him before that time. Or his god may even be devalued by the state!"

Money cannot buy salvation nor heaven.

Wealth cannot buy wisdom nor knowledge.

Wealth cannot buy health nor life when it is time to die. All the money in the world cannot buy one minute of life.

Wealth cannot buy love, and empty is the heart that lacks it.

Wealth cannot buy character.

Solomon, the richest man of his day, despaired of life and considered suicide! (Ecclesiastes 2:17).

THE POOR MAN WHO IS RICH

There is that maketh himself poor, yet hath great riches.—Proverbs 13:7

The man who has found Christ and knows Him as Saviour has discovered true riches. He has discovered the secret of life (Philippians 1:21; 3:7–11). He has entered into joy supreme. He has hope of heaven, and surety of the resurrection. He is a child of God and a member of the family of God. He has many Christian friends, and better yet, he has a friend that sticketh closer than a brother—Jesus Christ.

The Christian life is a life of service, living both for God and man, serving others. This is the key to true happiness. A rich reward awaits such a person in heaven.

God has promised to reward those who are faithful in life

and deed, so the Christian is constantly laying up treasures in
heaven (I Corinthians 3:12–15). What more could a Christian ask than to hear the words of his Lord, at the end of
life's journey, "Well done, thou good and faithful servant
Enter thou into the joy of the Lord."

The Christian not only has eternal life, he has entered
into the "more abundant life" (John 10:10).

A beggar's dead body was found on a park bench in
New York City's Central Park. Searching the pockets for
identity, the police discovered a strange piece of paper in
his pocket—his will! It read: "I give to all men who will
accept, the sun, the moon, the stars, the birds that sing,
the flowers, the trees, and the lake." Are we not all rich? The
rich are often poor, and the poor are exceedingly rich if
they have eyes to see, and ears to hear.

TRUE RICHES

*The ransom of a man's life are his riches; but the poor
heareth not rebuke.*—Proverbs 13:8

What are true riches? Let us consider values.

Proverbs 13:8 says that a rich man may be able to buy
his freedom (from a kidnapper), but the poor man never
needs to buy his freedom. What thief would rob him? He
is safe in his poverty! Sometimes it pays to be poor. The
poor are not cheated with gold; they enjoy true riches in-
deed.

Should we not list secondly, heaven? Think of a mansion
of gold on a street of gold. Jesus has gone to prepare a
place for you in heaven. Are you rich in heaven?

Eternal life is the greatest possession God could give to
man. What a privilege to live eternally. Jesus promised us
such life (John 11:25, 26).

Home, with children in it—this is true riches!

A church where we may worship and fellowship with
God and His people—this is true wealth.

Freedom—what a treasure! Health, provision, protection,
are worth much more than gold.

The Folly of Procrastination

DON'T DEFER SALVATION

Hope deferred maketh the heart sick: but when the desire cometh, it is a tree of life.—Proverbs 13:12

Hell is filled with people who have put off their salvation. More people are lost through procrastination than through any other contributing cause. There is very serious danger in delaying your decision to accept Christ as your Saviour.

The sinner is very apt to bargain for time and delay his decision to accept Christ by saying, "I'm not quite ready." Or else he may say, "I must think this over before I make a decision." Satan always encourages the sinner to delay making a decision to accept Christ, for this is his tactic to keep the sinner from actually being saved.

There is no good reason for putting off salvation. If your home were on fire and you were in danger of being burned alive, would you take time to sit and think it over before escaping from the burning house? Would you answer those who were attempting to save you, "I'm not quite ready yet"? Would you say, "There's no hurry. I must give this decision careful consideration, and this takes time. I refuse to be rushed. Some day, when I am older and have enjoyed this house to the fullest extent, then I will leave the burning house."

Of course you wouldn't! You would escape the burning house without a moment's delay. Why delay? Why take the risk of burning alive? And what is to be gained by putting off your salvation?

There are many reasons for not delaying your salvation. First, every day you delay, you lose another day of service for Jesus Christ, the one who died for you. Think of the good you could be doing if you were saved.

Second, every day you delay being a Christian, you lose

rewards in heaven. You cannot begin to lay up treasures in heaven until you are a Christian.

Third, the longer you live without Christ, the more sin you commit, the more you treasure up judgment against yourself. The longer you delay, the more entrenched you become in sin. Sins bind you with habits that will be harder to break each day you delay.

Fourth, you are using your influence either for good or for evil. If you are not saved, you are influencing others to be lost and to go the wrong way. Souls of your friends will go into eternity and eternal death because of your delay and influence upon them. You could have used your influence to bring them to God, but you yourself were not saved, and therefore you couldn't help them to God. Once they have died, it will be too late to witness to them. Your actions will be irrevocable. It may be some precious loved one who will be lost but who would have been saved.

Fifth, every day you delay, you harden your own heart in sin against God. You become the more entrenched in rebellion, unbelief, and sin. Pharaoh hardened his heart against God. Every opportunity to repent which he refused made his heart harder, until finally he reached the point of no return. So it is with the sinner. A tender heart soon becomes like steel through continuous rejection of Christ. The ear becomes deaf to God's voice through constant rejection. It is very dangerous to delay salvation.

Sixth, think of the blessings you will miss in this life every day you delay your salvation. A mission superintendent said to me when I was a boy, "Son, don't make the mistake I did. I was saved after I was fifty. I had already shortened my life with drink and sin, and now I must go to an early grave."

A radio newscaster said, "I wasted sixty-two years of my life without Christ. Now that I am saved, I realize that life doesn't begin until you know Christ as Saviour. Now my life is wasted and almost gone. Think what I missed by not being a Christian all these many years. Those years are lost forever!"

ACCEPT GOD'S WORD

Whoso despiseth the word shall be destroyed: but he that feareth the commandment shall be rewarded. The

*law of the wise is a fountain of life, to depart from
the snares of death.*—Proverbs 13:13, 14

Those who accept the Word of God and believe will be
saved. You ought to accept God's Word, simply because it
is the Word of God. God cannot lie. To reject His Word is
to make God a liar (I John 5:10). It is to rebel against
Him. Inasmuch as God has given you a revelation of truth,
what excuse do you have for not accepting it and being
saved? In the day of judgment, you will have no excuse
at all. God has not left you without light. You are not in the
darkness of ignorance. "Search the scriptures; for in them
ye think ye have eternal life: and they are they which testify
of me" (John 5:39).

We are born of the Word of God (I Peter 1:23). The
Scriptures are also able to make us wise unto salvation
(II Timothy 3:15). The Scriptures bring conviction, bringing us to God (Hebrews 4:12, 13). The Word gives us assurance of salvation (I John 5:13).

To ignore the Word of God is to leave yourself without
light, and if you are without light, you will be without
salvation (Hebrews 6:4–6).

You should heed the warnings of God and accept Christ
as your Saviour, because the Word of God is true. To reject
it or to ignore it is to reject truth. You then remain in
spiritual ignorance.

BOAST NOT THYSELF OF TOMORROW

*Boast not thyself of tomorrow; for thou knowest not
what a day may bring forth.*—Proverbs 27:1

Today you may be saved; tomorrow you may not have
this opportunity. Death may come very suddenly. Then salvation's door will close forever (Hebrews 9:27). The rich
fool said, "Eat, drink, and be merry; tomorrow I die." But
God answered, "Thou fool! This night (not tomorrow) thy
soul shall be required of thee." Boast not thyself of tomorrow; it may never come. "Now is the day of salvation" (II
Corinthians 6:2). While God is speaking to you, you should
hear and come (Hebrews 3:7, 8). Tomorrow you may
not hear His voice.

Life is uncertain. There is only one breath, one heart beat
between you and eternity. You may delay until you sleep in

peace, putting off your salvation, only to be suddenly called into eternity—forever! There is no chance for salvation after death (See Revelation 22:11; 14:10, 11; Luke 16:26–31).

The Value of Discipline

DISCIPLINE IS AN ACT OF LOVE

He that spareth the rod hateth his son: but he that loveth him chasteneth him betimes . . . Train up a child in the way he should go: and when he is old, he will not depart from it.—Proverbs 13:24; 22:6

Discipline does not mean beating! The word discipline is the same as disciple, or discipleship. To discipline a child is to teach him, to make him think as you think, do as you do, be as your are. It is to transplant your own ideas into the very being and fiber of the character of another. Disciples of Christ are those who are Christlike. This quality is attained by sitting at the feet of Jesus, by obeying His every word, by putting into action his very thoughts and views. To make a disciple of your child is to make him a carbon copy of you. Be sure the teacher makes a good pattern, however.

The use of the rod in discipline is an art (Proverbs 13:24). A parent who simply beats his child to give vent to his own anger does much more harm than good. He creates rebellion in the heart of the child, not discipleship. Use the rod when necessary, but *use it in love*. Let the child know that you do love him, but punish him wisely to correct error, or punish him for wrong doing. Try praying with your child before you punish him, and your chastisement will be more effective. Also your anger will subside. Never whip a child when angry.

More important than the rod is training (Proverbs 22:6). The word "train" means literally to catechise. That is, teach him the way. Make him memorize truth so that it becomes a part of his mind and being. Every time there is an advertisement for alcoholic beverages on television remind him of the evil effects of such stimulants. Show him the end result of drunkenness. Describe to him heart disease, cancer of the lungs and emphysema. Teach him until he hates evil.

83

Then he will be fortified against temptation, advertisemen and danger.

Teach your child the ten commandments. Have him mem orize the beatitudes, the Lord's prayer, the thirteenth chap ter of I Corinthians, the love chapter, and Romans 10:9 10 so he will know the plan of salvation. This is what means to train up a child. This is more than table manner though this too should be a part of his training. Pity th child who lacks such training and discipline.

DISCIPLINE SHOULD NOT BE DELAYED

Chasten the son while there is hope, and let not thy soul spare for his crying . . . The rod and reproof give wisdom: but a child left to himself bringeth his mother to shame . . . Correct thy son, and he shall give thee rest; yea he shall give delight unto thy soul.—Proverbs, 19:18; 29:15, 17

Training must begin early. A child learns more the fir two years of his life than throughout the remainder of h life. Early habits are lasting habits. It is easier to avoid a ba habit than to break a child of bad habits.

A child has much to learn, and it is easy for him misunderstand the importance of many of life's rules. Train ing should begin the moment a child is born. Never forge that much of what he learns is by watching you. You are h pattern, so make sure your life is proper.

If you wait until your child becomes a teen-ager to begi training him, it will be too late. The die will have cast b then. He should be encouraged to accept Christ as h Saviour early in life, and he should be taught the Bibl from his earliest years. Sin's strongest tug is during th years of youth, and he needs to be fortified against tempta tion.

The parent who loves his child so much that he will neithe correct nor punish him is doing the child no kindness. Suc a neglected child is doomed to trouble and failure, and th parent is sure to have a broken heart.

DISCIPLINE IS NECESSARY FOR ALL

Foolishness is bound in the heart of a child; but the rod of correction shall drive it far from him.—Proverbs 22:15

Everyone is born in sin. All have fallen nature. We all take after parents. It is necessary to correct a child, for he is allowed to follow his natural inclinations, they will lead him to ruin. He must be trained, taught, corrected, and sometimes gently punished. If we do not correct this natural inclination to sin and evil, the final result will be tragic.

A parent who allows a child to choose whether he will go to church or Sunday school is inviting disaster. A child needs spiritual help, and if it is neglected, he will come to ruin. God gave children parents to raise them because they need adults to guide them. Let them profit from our past experiences.

The natural inclination to evil can be broken through faithful training by the parents. But if the parents are indifferent and easygoing, the child will suffer in the end. He will grow up without faith, righteousness, and the strength and courage essential to successful living.

If a field is neglected and not cultivated, it will soon go to weeds. Weeds grow without encouragement; vegetables require cultivation. Flowers require much labor. So do good characters!

DISCIPLINE DELIVERS FROM HELL

Withhold not correction from the child: for if thou beatest him with the rod, he shall not die. Thou shalt beat him with the rod, and shalt deliver his soul from hell.—Proverbs 23:13, 14

Some fear the use of the rod. A child may cry, but if the parent is not cruel in punishing a child, the child will not be harmed physically, nor will he be scarred spiritually. A cruel beating of a child is wicked and criminal.

A child must learn that he must answer for his every act. This will teach him that he cannot steal, lie, or cheat and escape punishment. Unless you wish for your child to grow up with criminal tendencies, don't neglect discipline.

Chastisement may even make the difference in the eternal destiny of a child. A child must learn that sin cannot escape punishment on earth to teach him that God must also punish sin in the hereafter. Sin guilt will then drive him to Christ for the salvation of his soul.

Fools Mock Sin

THE TREACHERY OF SIN

Fools make a mock at sin: but among the righteous there is favour.—Proverbs 14:9

All men are sinners by nature. David wrote, "In sin di my mother conceive me" (Psalm 51:5). He did not mean that the act of conception was sin; he did mean that he wa born of sinful parents, and therefore he inherited a sinfu nature. Ephesians 2:3 says, "We were by nature the chil dren of wrath." The previous verses state that we were dead in trespasses and sins. This indicates that we were also sin ners by deed as well as by nature.

Some argue that it is not right or reasonable that they in herit sin from their parents just because Adam sinned Nevertheless, the fact remains that we are whatever ou parents were, for we cannot deny the fact of inheritance We might reason that it is not fair that we were born o poor parents, whereas others were born of rich parents, bu such an argument will make us none the richer!

Inasmuch as we are born sinners, a sinful deed is not th cause of our being sinners. A sinful act merely proves tha we are by nature sinners, otherwise the desire to sin woul not exist within us.

Thus we are twice guilty: by nature, and by deed.

God's wrath has already been revealed against all sin (Ro mans 1:18). His wrath was revealed on the cross whe God's judgment fell upon His Son in punishment for our sins God's wrath has also been revealed against sin in other in stances of divine judgment: the flood, the destruction o Sodom and Gomorrah, and the expulsion of Adam and Ev from the Garden of Eden.

Sinners will be judged according to their deeds (Roman 2:1–6). Many Scriptures warn of the judgment to come Luke 3:7; John 5:22; Acts 17:31; Revelation 20:11–15. Le

s take heed to the warning of God concerning judgment for
in.

Sinners will be punished for their sins unless they accept
he Saviour on the cross as a substitute for the punishment
f their sins.

Hebrews 9:27 makes clear the time of judgment—after
eath.

But thank God there is an escape from all judgment for
in. Christ took our judgment on the cross. If we will only
rust Him, asking forgiveness of sins, He can and will for-
ive. God as a just God cannot merely overlook sin because
Ie is sorry for us. Sin must be punished; justice demands
hat the penalty of the law must be paid. Therefore, it was
ecessary for Christ to become our substitute on the cross,
aking our punishment for us, so that He might forgive us.
ee Romans 4:7; 3:25; and 8:1.

Furthermore, Christ has broken the power of sin and set
s free from sin's servitude. Romans 6:14 assures us, "Sin
hall not have dominion (rule) over you." We are therefore
) reckon our old nature dead, and refuse to yield our mem-
ers as instruments of unrighteousness. (Romans 6:11–13).
in is inexcusable in the Christian life.

FOOLS MOCK SIN

Some foolishly say that sin does not even exist! They are
lind to murder, crime, violence, and wickedness that con-
umes the entire world. To ignore the lusts within our own
esh, and the temptation that exists is foolish. If we were
ot sinners, we could not be tempted. Sin is law breaking,
nd to deny sin is to deny law breaking.

The wages of sin is death, and all men die. Those who
ay there is no sin, or that they are not sinners will prove
heir claim to be false when they die.

Some go so far as to make sin gray, or white, rather than
lack. They justify sin, saying it is common to all men and
herefore is not wrong. But righteousness is not a variable
vhich is determined by common practice or opinion. Both
n and righteousness are absolutes which are set accord-
1g to the standards of the law of God. It is never wrong to
o right, and it is never right to do wrong. Righteousness is
ot determined by a code of convenience, dependent upon
uman excuse and reason. The end never justifies the means.
in is black—very black. There are no small sins. Sin is

rebellion against God. Sin nailed Jesus to a cross. Sin is wicked.

Some knowingly sin, ignoring consequences. They may even enjoy defying God's law. Rebellion is pleasure to them. Greater will be their punishment.

Some play with sin, boasting that they can break its habit at their own leisure. But sin deceives them. A man once tamed a cub lion and made a pet of it. It appeared to be perfectly harmless until it reached maturity. Then the lion turned against his trainer and killed him. Some excuse their sin and justify it, rather than to repent of their sin and acknowledge their evil. Sin is never justifiable. Sin is always wrong. To justify sin is to ignore the cross and the penalty Christ paid for sin.

FOOLS MAKE A MOCK OF THE SIN OFFERING

A careful translation of Proverbs 14:9 is: "Fools make a mock of the *sin offering*. This translation indicates that sinners often mock the sin offering, God's Son, Jesus Christ who died upon a cross for our sins. To reject Christ is to mock the sin offering and also the need of the sin offering.

A Confederate soldier was imprisoned and sentenced to be shot at sunrise. His father hastened to see Abraham Lincoln and pled for his son's life. Lincoln signed a pardon and gave it to the father. "Hurry," Lincoln said, "and deliver the pardon for the son before it is too late."

When the father arrived at the prison and presented the pardon, the officer in charge said, "You may personally deliver the pardon to your son in the prison cell."

The father ran down the corridors of the prison shouting "You don't have to die, son. I have a pardon for you." When he arrived at the son's cell he held the pardon for him to see. The boy reached through the bars, grabbed the pardon, tore it into shreds, cursing, and saying, "I won't accept a pardon signed by Abraham Lincoln!"

The next morning, there was a volley of shot in the nearby orchard, and the boy fell dead in his own blood. He didn't have to die. He had rejected his pardon. So it will be with the sinner who rejects God's pardon, which has been bought through the death of God's Son on the cross.

Man's Ways Are Not God's Ways

A WAY THAT SEEMETH RIGHT

There is a way which seemeth right unto a man, but the end thereof are the ways of death.—Proverbs 14:12

Man by human reason attempts to determine the plan of salvation. But salvation's plan has been determined by God and is revealed through divine revelation in the Word of God. To commit your soul's salvation to your own reason is dangerous. If man's opinion, which varies with individuals, is wrong, then your soul could be lost. We must make sure of our salvation. God's Word alone is worthy of our trust, and our assurance of salvation is based on the Word of God (I John 5:13).

When Naaman went to the prophet for healing and was told to go to the River Jordan and wash and be clean, he said, "I thought, He will surely come out to me, and call on the name of his God, and strike his hand over the place, and recover the leper." He further said he had better rivers than Jordan in Syria, and he suggested another way to be healed. But if he had been able to heal himself, why had he come to the prophet in the first place? His remedy was useless, as it didn't work. And the prophet's remedy hadn't been tried, though he criticized it. When the cure was applied it worked! That was all that counted.

So why not come God's way and be saved? Make sure!

Man's ways are many. Among them is the WAY OF SELF-RIGHTEOUSNESS. But God never speaks of man's righteousness. He speaks only of his unrighteousness (Romans 3:5). No man is righteous (Romans 3:10), therefore no man can be justified on the basis of his own righteousness (Romans 3:3–28).

Man has another way—SELF-JUSTIFICATION. Jesus referred to those who would justify themselves in Luke 18:9, when He gave the parable of the two men who prayed. The Pharisee justified himself by reciting his good works. The

Publican pled guilty and sought forgiveness. Which was justi
fied? The self-righteous Pharisee, or the repentant Publican?
The Publican, of course. So it is today. Those who confess
their sins find salvation and are justified in the sight of God.
The self-righteous die in their sins.

Then there is the WAY OF GOOD WORKS. Some would
attempt to get to heaven on the basis of their good deeds,
but no matter how good they are, or how much good they
may do, they still are sinners by nature and need salvation.
Regardless of how much good they may do, their good
deeds cannot undo the sin they have already committed. We
are saved by grace, apart from works, through faith (Romans 3:28; Ephesians 2:8–10; II Timothy 1:9; Titus 3:5).

Others seek salvation through RELIGIOUS CERE-
MONY. They attempt to wash away their sins with the
waters of baptism. Or they trust in communion or church
membership to wash away their sins. But only the blood of
Christ can cleanse the heart of the sinner, and only God's
transforming power can change the nature of man through
regeneration resulting in a new birth (John 3:3, 5). We are
not saved by ritual, but by a new birth (Galatians 6:15).

There are those who would be saved by KEEPING THE
TEN COMMANDMENTS. The ten commandments prove
that we are guilty and condemn us; they do not atone for
our guilt (Galatians 3:10–12). The commandments weren't
given to save, but to guide those who are already saved, that
they might be a special perfection both in the nature and
deed; therefore we cannot be saved by the law, but only by
grace (Romans 10:1–10).

A WAY THAT LEADS TO DESTRUCTION AND IS WRONG

*There is a way that seemeth right unto a man, but the
end thereof are the ways of death.*—Proverbs 14:12

"The wages of sin is death." Unless sin is forgiven, the
penalty is inescapable (Romans 6:23). All are sinners, so
we must all seek forgiveness through the blood of Christ, or
else we must die eternally. God will destroy the wicked forever (Psalm 52:5). Spiritual death is not cessation of existence, but rather eternal existence shut out from the presence of God forever.

God warned Israel of the punishment because of sin, and
the same principle applies to us today (Jeremiah 13:25;
48:6–8).

Romans 5:12–21 warns us that sin brought spiritual death upon all men, but Jesus Christ brought life eternal.

Jesus warned in John 8:21–24 that those who died without a Saviour because of unbelief would die without hope of salvation.

Shall we not take heed of our lost condition and seek a Saviour?

Sin is a disease of the soul. To neglect this disease means certain death. If one had cancer, he would seek medical aid, lest he should die. Why ignore the lost condition of your soul? There is a sure cure. There is salvation for those who will seek God's help and salvation. Then why not come to Christ and believe and be saved?

GOD'S WAY IS THE WAY OF LIFE

What a precious promise is John 3:16—"shall not perish but have everlasting life." We may escape eternal death. We may enter into eternal life. Eternal life is God's life. By accepting Christ as our Saviour, we are born into the family of God, and become partakers of the divine nature of God (II Peter 1:4), sharing His life which is eternal. We shall never die (John 11:25, 26).

As soon as we trusted in Christ, we entered into salvation and received the Holy Spirit as our eternal companion and guide. We entered into the inheritance of God's children, became a member of God's family, and became a son of God with all of its benefits (Ephesians 1:13–14).

To have the Son of God in our hearts is to have eternal life. Not to have the Son of God is to be without life, and to dwell in the shadow of eternal death (I John 5:12). In other words, if you have the Son of God within your heart, sometime and in some definite place, you received Christ as your Saviour. If you have the Son, you invited Him into your heart. Did you? You either have the Son, or else you do not. This is no guess work! (I John 5:11–13).

God's way is the best way, for it delivers from sin and punishment, and it also imparts a new life to us. It gives us absolute assurance of heaven and spiritual security. Jesus said, "I am the WAY" (John 14:6). Man's way is the wrong way. Jesus Christ is the one and only WAY.

The Backslider

The backslider in heart shall be filled with his own ways: and a good man shall be satisfied from himself.
—Proverbs 14:14

THE HEART IS THE SOURCE OF SIN

Much spiritual instability exists among Christians today. Few are grounded and solid in their Christian profession and life. So few are in fellowship with God, and so few have spiritual power. This is due largely to a lack of dedication to Christ and an infilling of the Holy Spirit. Too many Christians are saved, and that is all. They have never fully yielded themselves to Christ as we are urged to do in Romans 12:1-2.

This spiritual lack is due chiefly to a failure to read the Bible and to study its truths. Prayerlessness is a contributing factor. We grow strong spiritually only as we feed upon the Bread of Life. Weak Christians are very easily tempted, or else they are swept off their feet by every wind of false doctrine. Temptations of our day are greater than ever before, but Christians who are fortified with a deeper knowledge of the truth and complete dedication to Christ cannot be fazed by modern temptation. The winds may blow, and the floods may come, but those who have built their house upon the rock, Christ Jesus, will withstand the storm and attacks of Satan.

Our difficulty is *heart trouble*. The natural heart of man is desperately wicked beyond belief. If our heart is right with God, and fully yielded to Christ, then good will come forth not evil (Luke 6:45). The Bible speaks of those who have a double heart, or a divided heart. Such are easily led astray.

Our Lord uncovered a cockatrice den within the heart of man (Matthew 15:18–20). The eggs of sin are within the heart, and they will hatch out into horrible sins if the heart is not purified. That is why Proverbs 14:14 speaks of a backslider's heart. The need of purification within is our

92

greatest need today. The lack of love, of service, and deed is due to sin hidden within the heart of men. Some think hidden sins cannot be seen and are therefore unimportant. But if the inner heart of man is unsound, his spiritual life will be cold and empty. The reason there is so little spiritual enthusiasm and love among Christians is a backslidden heart.

The inner nature of man will reveal itself with deeds (Matthew 7:17, 18). Make sure your heart is right with God. We are told in Romans 10:10 that with the heart man believes. Romans 10:9 says we are to confess that Christ Jesus is Lord of our life. To be Lord, the heart must receive Him and enthrone Him.

SIN BRINGS ITS OWN RETRIBUTION

(Isaiah 1:4–6; Hebrews 12:6–11)

The prodigal son in Luke 15:11–24 soon became filled with his own ways. He came to want. He repented and admitted that he had played the fool. His father's servants were better off then he was. He had lost his father's fellowship and blessings, and found himself in a pig pen, feeding the swine, but no man gave anything to him. All prodigals sooner or later come to want. They are soon filled with their own ways. There is no joy in backsliding.

A state policeman in Pennsylvania was taken to a hospital. He was extremely ill, but the doctor could not find the cause of his fever and sent for the minister. The doctor said to the minister, "I think his trouble must be spiritual; it is not physical."

As the minister read to the policeman from Isaiah 53, "He was wounded for our transgressions, he was bruised for our iniquities: the chastisement of our peace was upon him; and with his stripes we are healed. All we like sheep have gone astray; we have turned every one to his own way; and the Lord hath laid on him the iniquity of us all," the policeman began to weep. Then he revealed his story. He was a minister's son, backslidden, and living in sin. As soon as he prayed and sought forgiveness, his fever was gone.

The minister phoned his parents, who lived in Tennessee, and reported to them that their son had come back to the Lord. There was a glorious reunion, and great joy filled their hearts.

Isaiah pled with Israel, asking them why they should suffer more punishment from God because of their sins. He

beckoned them to return to the Lord and find forgivenes
and joy. God always offers forgiveness and restoration t
those who will return. But He warns us in His Word tha
the way of the transgressor is hard.

Out of love God chastens us when we are out of His will
when we are sinful, or forgetful. The Psalmist said, "He
restoreth my soul" (Psalm 23:3). Spurgeon commented, "
am glad He restores my soul, for when I am out of the wil
of God, my heart becomes cold and indifferent. I would
never return to Him, so He goes after me and restores me."

Our Father does not enjoy chastening us, nor do we enjoy
being chastened, but if it were not for the faithful rebuke
and chastening of the Lord, we would be satisfied in our
coldness and backsliding. (See Hebrews 12:6–11).

THE REPENTANCE OF THE BACKSLIDER

(Psalm 51: I John 1:9; 2:3)

When the prodigal son had enough of sin and its sorrows,
he vowed he would return to his father and ask forgiveness.
He would ask only to take the place of a servant, for he
thought he was no longer worthy to be called a son. But
when he returned home, he found his father watching for
him, and ready both to forgive and to restore him as a son.
He put a ring of authority upon his finger and clothed him
in new garments (typical of our righteousness in Christ) and
killed the fatted calf, to make merry. There is joy in heaven
over one sinner who repents. If you are out of fellowship
with God, come back home. A warm welcome awaits you!

In Psalm 51, David confessed his terrible sins of adultery
and murder. He acknowledged his sin, confessed it, and
sought forgiveness. There is no hope of forgiveness until we
do acknowledge our need. Then only will we confess our
sin and seek forgiveness. We have the promise of God in
I John 1:9, "If we confess our sins, he is faithful and just to
forgive us our sins, and to cleanse us from *all* unrighteousness." God stands ready to forgive any and all who will
repent and return to Him.

A True Witness

A true witness delivereth souls: but a deceitful witness speaketh lies.—Proverbs 14:25

WE ARE THE SINNER'S BIBLE

R. G. LeTourneau said, "What we need are more demonstrators of Christianity." How true!

The average Mr. Pagan seldom goes to church. He does not believe the Bible; he is not interested. He is taught the theory of evolution from the moment he enters school. He is taught that he does not need God, for evolution tells him that the world came by accident.

He is being constantly bombarded with materialism, atheism, communism, and unbelief. He is demoralized with pornography and sex is glorified until it takes the place of God. If he flees for strength to resist the onslaught of godlessness to religion, he is disillusioned and frustrated by modern theologians who tell him that God is dead!

The end result is that it is almost impossible to talk to him about his soul. He has become self-satisfied, and he considers the Christian who lives next door to be harmless but peculiar, and mentally sick. He has never been brought face to face with eternity. He knows he will die someday, but he refuses to think about it. He is doing as he pleases, and he doesn't wish to be disturbed.

Just how can we reach Mr. Pagan? How can we awaken him to the danger of his situation? How can we make him conscious that he is a sinner and that he needs a Saviour? He doesn't believe in a hell, nor in in the deity of Christ, nor in the Bible. What can we do to convince him that there is a heaven to win and a hell to shun? How may we prove to him that Jesus Christ is more than a religious leader and prophet, and truly God and Saviour?

Shall we invite Mr. Pagan to church? Will he go? He might, but the chances are he will excuse himself from going. Or else he will promise to go, but when the time to go arrives, he will arrange some emergency to excuse himself from his engagement. You may try inviting him, but don't be surprised if he disappoints you. If you have already awakened his conscience, then he might go; otherwise he will not.

The truth is, YOU ARE THE SINNER'S BIBLE! You, and you alone, can awaken his conscience. The life you live is a silent witness. He is watching your every act, mood, and word. He is observing to see if there is anything different about you. If you are no better than he, then he will not be impressed with the value of your confession of Christ. He is watching to see if you are happier and more victorious over trouble than he. If your profession of faith is real and is reflected in your daily life, then you may be able to talk to him and to explain your Christian faith. Eventually, you may be able to persuade him to go to church with you to learn more of the more abundant and worthwhile life.

We are *witnesses with our lips,* also. Mr. Pagan is listening to our every word. What you say reveals what you are, what you really think. You may tell Mr. Pagan that you have faith, but if he observes you worrying, he will not believe you. You may tell him you have hope in death, but he watches to see how you act at a funeral. If you do not have victory over sorrow, he will disdain your profession.

We witness with our deeds. If you shortchange the baker, the butcher, and the groceryman, he will conclude that you and your faith are a fraud. If you have the same bad habits he does, he will conclude that you have nothing to offer him, for he is as good as you are.

We may also *witness with the printed page.* A tract or a printed sermon may reach him in secret in his home. Use tracts; be constantly busy giving printed pamphlets to sinners. The communists print and distribute beautiful magazines and literature by the billions, enough for every living person on earth to receive at least six or seven copies a year. Should we not be even more alert and active in spreading truth?

We witness with our attitude. If we are unkind, inconsiderate, ungracious, lacking in good manners, the sinner will disdain our Christianity. The only Christ he knows is the Christ in you. If you are critical, filled with hate, jealousy, meanness, and nastiness, then Mr. Pagan will conclude that Christ is that way, for He dwells within your heart, and produces the Christian life in you.

A True Christian Life Wins Souls

The sinner is hungry. When Christ taught the beatitudes, He was looking into the faces of disillusioned, sick, and hungry people. They were heartbroken. The sinner is the same today. He is hungry for something, but he does not know what. He does not have the answer. He is tired of war, killing, hate, insecurity, disappointments, and heartaches. His pleasure has failed him, and he has discovered life is empty! He may have tried religion, only to find it did not satisfy his heart's longing. The true Christian has found the answer; he must share his great discovery with Mr. Pagan.

The sinner is sick with a soul disease—sin. It has steadily destroyed him, body, soul, and spirit. He is shocked at the results of sin. He can't understand why he does the things he does. He needs Christ. Tell him!

The sinner is in danger of eternal hell. Warn him. How can you be silent? He has sorrow and no comfort, so share with him the God of all comfort. He has no hope for the future, after death, or eternity. Christ is his only hope. Tell him. Sin has overcome him, and he cannot do what is right, try as hard as he will. Jesus is the great deliverer. His life is empty. Christ will fill this vacuum and make life worth living. You must share Jesus with others. You dare not remain silent.

A False Christian Life Hinders the Gospel

Can you preach deliverance from sin if you are a slave to some evil habit? Can you expose sin when you cherish it? Can you tell the sinner he needs to be saved if your own life has not been changed? Can you tell him to worship Christ, if Satan rules in your heart? Dare you preach love and practice hate? Love is the very essence of Christianity; do you love? The sinner is watching you! Your life is always witnessing— either for Christ, or else against Christ. You are either bringing men to Christ, or else you are driving them away.

The Fear of the Lord

FEAR OF THE LORD IS CONFIDENCE

In the fear of the Lord is strong confidence: and his children shall have a place of refuge.—Proverbs 14:26

The expression, "fear of the Lord," occurs often in th book of Proverbs. It means literally: reverence, devotion worship, and trust. It is indicative of the faith which th New Testament refers to in reference to the saving faith The expression indicates that you are dwelling in the Lord and your life is a Christian life, filled with meditation an communion with God.

The fear of the Lord, we are told, is a source of inne strength. The person who lives this life of faith and devotio is able to meet the tests of time, and to meet the shocks o life.

A minister who had spoken six times one Easter Sunda was so weary when he arose to speak the last time that h felt he could not do so. He prayed and asked God fo strength. To his amazement, as he spoke, God did strength en him, and when he was finished speaking, he felt refreshe and rested.

A Christian who had lost his precious mother prayed fo strength, and God gave both strength and comfort. "It wa miraculous," he said.

A Christian who was going to the operating room, re peated Isaiah 40:29-31, "He giveth power to the faint; an to them that have no might he increaseth strength. Eve youths shall faint and be weary, and the young men sha utterly fall: But they that wait upon the Lord shall rene their strength; they shall mount up with wings as eagles; the shall run, and not be weary; and they shall walk, and no faint."

Not only did the Lord strengthen her, but the docto heard her repeating these words, and he said after the o eration, "I never performed an operation where all was s against me. I would have lost her on the operating table, but I could feel the presence of the Lord. He guided my hand, and He gave me strength, too."

In Judges 15:16–18, we read that Samson slew 1000 Philistines with the jaw bone of an ass. He was so exhausted and weary that he cried for water, and God opened a spring, and he drank and was refreshed. This is a spiritual illustration of the inner strength that God gives to those who fear the Lord. The inner strength does not depend upon an outside influence, or drugs. This is the Spirit of the Lord within us. As the angels ministered to Elijah after his conflict with the prophets of Baal and Jezebel, so Christ ministers to us. As the angels ministered to Christ after the temptation, the Holy Spirit ministers to us.

In I John 4:4 we are given the secret of this inner strength: the Christ within us is greater than Satan or any enemy without in the world. The inner power exceeds the outer enemy. How can we be defeated?

Proverbs 14:26 further promises that the children of the Christian live in security and find refuge from their fears and worries. Children raised in a godless home often lack a sense of security and peace. They are affected psychologically throughout life with insecurity. Faith pays big dividends!

THE FEAR OF THE LORD IS A FOUNTAIN OF LIFE

The fear of the Lord is a fountain of life, to depart from the snares of death.—Proverbs 14:27

The fountain of life is often referred to in Scripture. Isaiah speaks of drawing water at the wells of salvation (Isaiah 12:3). The children of Israel drank water from the rock, Christ Jesus, at Rephidim, a desert place (Exodus 17:1–7). God led them through the wilderness into Elim where there were twelve fountains of water (Exodus 15:27). We read that in Palestine Abram was a well digger, and his son Isaac cleaned out the wells the Philistines had filled up with debris which had clogged them up and caused the waters to cease to flow. All of these figures indicate that the Christian has a source of spiritual water.

Always water in Scripture is indicative of salvation, and the new life which surges within the Christian. In the gospel of John, water symbolizes the new life within, which is the result of the Holy Spirit within us. John 7:37–39 defines water clearly. In John 4:10, 13, 14, the woman of Sycar is

promised eternal life, which is compared to waters of life
In the first epistle of John, the figure of water still continue
with the same meaning—the new life of the Christian. (
John 5:6, 8).

Our text, Proverbs 14:27, assures us that those who fea
the Lord will have this eternal life within, and it will fortify
them against death and eternal loss. What a precious prom
ise! It pays to be a Christian!

THE FEAR OF THE LORD IS BETTER THAN WEALTH

*Better is little with the fear of the Lord than great
treasure and trouble therewith.*—Proverbs 15:16

What would you do if you had to choose between your
life and one million dollars? Or even one billion dollars? Or
shall we raise the price for your soul to all the wealth of the
entire world? Your answer is easy—you would choose life
over wealth. Then, would you use the same judgment when
it comes to choosing between eternal life and money?

A wealthy businessman once said he had chosen money
instead of God. He could not give up his wealth. And yet, he
was dead within a few days after he said that! He did give
up all of his money and wealth when he died, anyway.

When the Titanic was sinking, a wealthy Philadelphia
broker stood on board the sinking ship, watching the life
boats pull away from the sinking ship. He cried out, "I'l
give five million dollars to anyone who will give me his place
in the life boat!"

A young man answered, "Keep your millions! What good
will they be when you are dead?"

Yes, what good is wealth when you must choose between
it and eternal life? A rich ruler came to Jesus and made a
choice between Christ and his wealth. He chose wealth. He
has long since been dead, and his wealth perished with him.

Righteousness Exalteth a Nation

HOW RIGHTEOUSNESS EXALTETH A NATION

Righteousness exalteth a nation: but sin is a reproach to any people.—Proverbs 14:34

There are seven reasons why righteousness exalteth a nation. First, *Righteousness is the basis of health for a nation.* Some years ago a study was made on the history of a nation which has never become strong and great. We endeavored to discover why. The nation has great resources and a perfect climate. The ethnic background of the people is excellent. The cause of their poverty and lack of progress was accidentally stumbled upon. The country is disease-ridden. Venereal disease has destroyed the health of the nation.

Because of poor health, the people do not have the will to work. Many are unemployed, and many lack the will power to create or produce. The country has suffered greatly economically.

Back of the poor health of the people is a lack of faith. The people had religion to some extent, but true salvation which changes the lives and morals of people had never been preached.

Secondly, *righteousness is the basis of the home.* A country without faith lacks the power to cement the family into a permanent unit. Ownership by land occupants is most important to the economy of any country. And the family must be permanently united to accomplish this. Love for country and loyalty depend upon family unity.

Third, *righteousness is the basis of morality.* A person without faith has no incentive to live a good life. A lack of fear of judgment and punishment for wrongdoing produces careless living. Sin robs man of a desire to live righteously; he does not expect a reward. Therefore, he deteriorates morally and lives dissolutely. Paul wrote his epistle to the Romans warning them of the moral decay of Rome, and revealed the final decay and destruction of the Roman Empire if they did not seek God and have faith. It is even so today. Unbelief destroys a nation from within.

Fourth, *righteousness is the basis of patriotism, and loyalty*. The family that worships together in the house of God on the Lord's day has a sense of loyalty that does not exist in the heart of an irreligious person. Religion is the cornerstone of patriotism. Those who burn our flag are not those who worship the Lord in church on Sunday. False religion destroys this loyalty to God, nation, or mankind.

Fifth, *righteousness is the basis of faith and tranquility*. A person lacking faith is disturbed emotionally and is apt to become a source of trouble. Civil strife is never stirred up by true Christians, but by those who don't truly know God. They may have a false religion which gives them no hope, and they will cause strife. But the true believer in Christ is peaceful. He believes in love and not violence.

Sixth, *righteousness is the basis of wealth*. A person who lives a righteous life is frugal, industrious, and productive. An immoral person gambles, wastes his wealth, and fails to produce wealth. Love of God and family is an incentive to labor.

Seventh, *righteousness is the basis of human progress*. A righteous person enjoys working. His job is part of his very life. He is not easily misled by troublemakers who make a practice of fomenting labor trouble. He has certain moral principles which force him to deal fairly with his employer.

SIN IS A REPROACH TO ANY NATION

It is an abomination to kings to commit wickedness: for the throne is established by righteousness.—Proverbs 16:12

Just as righteousness exalts a nation, the opposite is true. Sin is a reproach to a nation.

First, sin produces crime. Crime eats out the very life of a nation until law and government is destroyed. We are constantly being warned that as the army of criminals increases, we will soon reach a stage of anarchy in which government itself will be destroyed. Each year the crime rate increases. The average criminal age is nineteen. Ninety percent of crime is committed by youth between the ages of nineteen and twenty-one. More than six million people have a criminal record in the United States, and this army of criminals is increasing daily. Law and order will soon be unable to cope with crime unless there is a spiritual revival, and a turning to God in Christian faith.

Daily it is becoming more unsafe to be on the streets of most of our cities. Hotels are becoming dangerous. Innocent people are being raped and murdered in their homes. Riots and strife are increasing. Our only hope is revival. We must turn to God as a nation.

Second, immorality dissipates our national strength. Many youths are unfit for military service because of a life of sin and dissipation. Many have given themselves over to dope, liquor, and sex sins, until their health is broken. Our nation is being weakened by our enemy who entices our youth into these sins.

Godlessness produces lawlessness. False ideologies produce riots, eventually revolution. Sadly enough, we have ruled the Bible and prayer out of the schools at a time when we should be seeking God. And yet, we have retained the athestic, communistic theory of evolution which denies the Bible account of creation, undermining faith in God's Word. Furthermore, sin produces political corruption. It destroys faithfulness which is the basis for all business transactions. And eventually, sin will destroy our personal liberty.

THE END OF THE NATION THAT FORGETS GOD

The wicked shall be turned into hell, and all the nations that forget God.—Psalm 9:17

History proves that every nation that forgets God crumbles and disappears. Rome is an example. Rome was not defeated by an outside enemy; it crumbled within. God removes His blessing from the nation that forgets Him. Israel and Judah are examples of this. They went into captivity, though warned of God, when they turned to idolatry. Sin always brings its own retribution! Our nation will soon be cast into hell unless we repent and return to God.

As one person recently said, "If judgment doesn't soon fall upon America, God will have to apologize to Sodom and Gomorrah for having destroyed them when they were less sinful!

Thy God Seeth Thee

There are three natural attributes which are peculiar to and limited to deity. They are omniscience, omnipotence, and omnipresence. Omniscience means that God knows all. Omnipotence indicates that God is all powerful; there is nothing He cannot do. Omnipresence means that God is everywhere. These attributes belong alone to deity. Christ claimed and demonstrated these three attributes, for He was God as well as man.

GOD KNOWS ALL

The thoughts of the wicked are an abomination to the Lord: but the words of the pure are pleasant words. —Proverbs 15:26

God knows our very thoughts. Nothing is hid from Him. Both sin and righteousness begin in the mind. We think always before we act. As a man thinketh, so is he. What we do merely reveals what we are. Thought always precedes sin. All of us have evil thoughts, and some think that it is not wrong to think evil as long as they do not do evil. But evil thinking is the first step to sin, and an evil mind pollutes the soul. Be careful what you read, what you see, for thoughts are hatched through the eye gate.

God also knows our evil deeds. There is no perfect crime, for God sees everything we do. He keeps a record of our deeds, and we will be judged accordingly. Every man shall be judged for his works (I Corinthians 3:13). Always remind yourself that God knows your deeds even if no one else does.

God knows our motives. We are expert in excusing our sins and in justifying our wrong doings. But God knows what our real motive is. We cannot excuse our sins before God's judgment bar. He knows how much we love, and how much we hate.

God knows our intended plans. That is why in the Sermon

on the Mount Jesus taught that He would judge men not according to the law, but according to their evil designs before evil acts were committed. Isaiah 11:3 states that Christ will judge "not after the sight of the eyes, neither reprove after the hearing of the ears: but with righteousness he shall judge." He will not judge by circumstantial evidence, for He knows the intents of the hearts of men.

God knows our hearts. Jealousy, hate, malice, envy, are wicked and related sins. They smoulder in the heart of man. God knows they exist, hidden away in our hearts.

God knows whether we are sincere or insincere. Hypocrisy is worthless, for God knows whether you mean what you say or do.

GOD SEES ALL

The eyes of the Lord are in every place, beholding the evil and the good.—Proverbs 15:3

Psalm 139 enlarges upon the truth of this verse. Read it carefully.

God is everywhere. How foolish it was for Jonah to attempt to run from the presence of the Lord. If you fly ten miles above the earth, God is there. In space, He is there. In hell, He is there. All things live and move, and have their being in Him. In Him all things consist and hold together. Go to the ends of the earth, He is there. He sees all. He watches you.

Darkness will not hide you from God. There is a new ray of black light which makes men visible even though they move in the dark. An enemy can be seen with this light, and yet he does not know he is being watched. God made that ray of light! That God sees everything you do.

There is no hiding place; no place to which you may escape. When men stand before Christ to be judged, they will have no place of escape. Heaven and earth itself will have fled away. Regardless, God is everywhere anyway.

God knows all. He sees the sparrow fall. That is, He sees a small bird set his wings and glide in the air. He counts the hairs on your head. Is it not conforting that God cares for even the sparrows, and you know He cares for you. Are you not worth more than sparrows? He sees and knows your every need.

God hears our prayers, for He is always present. Is it not wonderful that God sees us when we kneel before Him in penitence? Or when we cry out in the time of trouble, He sees our difficulties. When the disciples were in a storm on the sea, rowing helplessly, getting nowhere, Christ was on a mountain praying for them. He came walking on the sea, to aid them. He still prays for us, watches us, and comes to aid in the time of need.

GOD WILL JUDGE ALL

If thou sayest, Behold, we knew it not; doth not he that pondereth the heart consider it? and he that keep-eth thy soul, doth not he know it? and shall not he render to every man according to his works? Hell and destruction are before the Lord: how much more then the hearts of the children of men?—Proverbs 24:12; 15:11

All men know that God is the Creator of the universe and all that dwell therein. He is a moral God, for He gave man a conscience. If God wrote a law in our hearts, a conscience, then He will also bring us into judgment, and if we are to be judged, then there must be a place of punishment.

Christ is to be our judge. This is made clear in Acts 17:31, and in John 5:22.

The judgment of the sinner is described in Revelation 20:11–15. The sinner is lost even now, before he dies, but he will be raised after death to be judged, so final sentence may be passed upon him. His guilt is precluded, because he has rejected or neglected the Saviour, Jesus Christ. He will be punished according to his deeds.

The judgment of the Christians will be for the sake of rewards (II Corinthians 5:10).

Men will be judged for their deeds (Romans 2:6).

Men will be judged for every idle word (Matthew 12:36).

Men will be judged for every evil thought (I Corinthians 4:5).

Peacemakers

A SOFT ANSWER

A soft answer turneth away wrath: but grievous words stir up anger.—Proverbs 15:1

What would our Lord Jesus Christ do under attack? Would He have fought back? Did He quarrel with His enemies? Paul wrote to Timothy, "Jesus Christ witnessed a good confession before Pontius Pilate" (I Timothy 6:13). And what did Jesus say to Pilate when He was falsely accused by His enemies? He answered not a word, and Pilate marvelled at His silence. He asked Him if He did not hear what his accusers said. Isaiah wrote concerning the Messiah, "As a sheep before her shearers is dumb, so he openeth not his mouth" (Isaiah 53:7). So we may conclude that a soft answer is Christlike. If you would be like your Lord, reply softly to your critics.

We are admonished, "Be not overcome of evil, but overcome evil with good" (Romans 12:21). If we answer our enemies with bitter words, then we are as wicked as our enemies. Do not stoop to their level. Two wrongs never make right one wrong. You may be attacked and bitterly accused or misrepresented. It is better to turn the other cheek than to strike back. Don't make yourself as bad as your enemy.

Vengeance is sinful. God retaliates against sin. That is His business—not yours (Romans 12:18, 19). Vengeance on your part is to take God's law into your own hands. He is the judge of the universe, not you. If your enemy hungers, feed him (Romans 12:20). Return good for evil. If he thirsts, give him water. Show kindness for unkindness and thus conquer your enemies.

Someone criticized Abraham Lincoln because he was not harsh with his enemies and critics. Replied Lincoln, "Can you think of a better way to conquer your enemies than to make them your friends through kindness?"

Christ taught us to love our enemies. He told us to return good for evil. We are to pray for our enemies. This is contrary to the world, but it is becoming to the Christian. Christ taught us the law of the second mile. If your enemy forces you to walk a mile, then walk two! (Matthew 5:38-39). If we are Christians we have no choice but to obey the commands of our Lord. Nevertheless, the principle of love which Christ taught is practical. If all men and all governments practiced His teachings, what a happy and prosperous world this would be!

Strife genders strife; quietness genders peace. It requires two people to have a quarrel. If one will not quarrel, the other will soon give up the fight. A Quaker returned his neighbor's cow for the twentieth time, from his cornfield. Said the Quaker to his godless neighbor, "If thy cow breaks into my cornfield again, I will . . . ."

The godless neighbor interrupted with scorn, "Just what will you do?"

"I shall return him to thee again," said the Quaker. The cow never again broke into the Quaker's cornfield.

When you answer your foe and quarrel with him, hate deepens, and the fires of hatred burst into open flame. It becomes most difficult to put them out, once they reach the stage of conflagration.

Grievous words breed hate, envy, and jealousy. Pride adds fuel to the fire. Would it not be far better to quietly overlook your critic's words? After all, words cannot really hurt you if you ignore them. It is pride and envy that cause an enemy to attack you, so why hurt his pride? Pray that he will overcome this evil in his nature.

SLOW TO ANGER

A wrathful man stirreth up strife: but he that is slow to anger appeaseth strife.—Proverbs 15:18

Strife is like a fire. If you add kindling to it, it will burn the faster and the more furiously. It will grow hotter, and it will spread. The Chicago fire began with a match! Don't add fuel to the fires of hate by pouring on volatile words which are like gunpowder or gasoline. Stop the fire when it is a small flame. It is much easier to put out a match than a burning city. When you answer with words of hate that are inflammatory, the fires will spread and hurt many innocent people.

Problems will solve themselves if left alone. The more you try to solve a problem by fighting back at your enemies, the worse it will become. If you leave it alone, the fires will soon die out. It will be easier to allay the fears of your enemy and change his hate into love through words of understanding and wisdom, than by inflaming him with argument. The more you say, the more adamant he will become, and the more entrenched your enemy will be in hate. Return roses to your enemy when he throws hand grenades.

Strife destroys churches, governments, and people. One quarrelsome person can cause an entire church to cease to labor for Christ. It was Nehemiah who replied to his enemy, Sanballat, "I am doing a great work, so that I cannot come down: Why should the work cease while I leave it, and come down to you?" (Nehmiah 6:3). Nothing pleases Satan more than to occupy God's servants with quarreling, so they cease to win souls. People who fight each other never fight the devil! People who quarrel get ulcers as a reward for their evil doing.

Strife causes bloodshed and suffering. Is it not much better to forgive than to quarrel?

BE NOT HASTY IN SPIRIT

He that is slow to wrath is of great understanding: but he that is hasty of spirit exalteth folly. The heart of the righteous studieth to answer: but the mouth of the wicked poureth out evil things.—Proverbs 14:29; 15:28

Don't jump to conclusions. There are two sides to every story. Never pass judgment until you have heard both sides. You may condemn an innocent person who needs sympathy instead of criticism if you are hasty in passing judgment.

Always consider the consequences of what you say. Better not say anything than to speak and cause harm and not good. The fact a thing is true does not give you license to repeat it.

Weigh carefully your words before you speak. Make every word pass through three gates: One, is this true? Two, is it kind for me to repeat it? Three, will I help the person involved if I repeat it?

As a Christian make the habit of lifting up the fallen, not pushing him down because he has made a mistake.

A Comparison of Values

LITTLE WITH GOD IS BETTER THAN TREASURES

Better is little with the fear of the Lord than great treasure and trouble therewith.—Proverbs 15:16

A jewelry salesman will always cast a diamond upon a black or deep purple velvet background to reveal its true beauty. Contrast is essential to reveal the full value of anything. To establish the value of property, or jewels, comparison must be made with known values. So it is that Proverbs constantly compares values of things that are common in life, so that we may fully appreciate Christian character, to encourage us to choose right. Let us carefully consider a comparison of these values, selecting eight such comparisons.

LITTLE WITH GOD IS BETTER THAN TREASURES

Better is a dinner with herbs where love is, than a stalled ox and hatred therewith.—Proverbs 15:17

The banquet table was spread sumptuously. Decorations were gorgeous. Famous people gathered to dine and feast. However hatred flared like a hot furnace, and jealousy raged within the hearts of those who sought honor one above another. The guests hardly were conscious of their environment, nor were they conscious of what they ate. Many suffered from indigestion afterward.

In contrast, at a home in Grand Rapids, a godly family stood about the table and sang hymns. Then they clasped hands and prayed. During the meal, which was simple and plain, they talked about the Lord and discussed precious Bible truths. It was a little bit of heaven on earth.

Visitors in this home were conscious that they had been in heaven! The Christian home is heaven on earth.

RIGHTEOUSNESS VERSUS REVENUE

Better is a little with righteousness than great revenues without right.—Proverbs 16:18

There was a rich man who fared sumptuously. He was dressed in purple. A poor beggar lay at his gate full of sores, and the dogs licked his sores. Both men died. The poor man was comforted in Abraham's bosom, but the rich man lifted up his eyes in hell, being in torments! (Luke 16:19–31). Which of these two men would you choose to be? This incident does not teach us that it is evil to be rich, nor good to be poor. Nor does it teach that poverty is the road to heaven, and riches the way to hell. But it does teach us that if we must choose between riches and heaven, it would be better to be poor and go to heaven. If you must make a choice, choose heaven!

WISDOM IS BETTER THAN GOLD

How much better it is to get wisdom than gold! and to get understanding rather to be chosen than silver!—Proverbs 16:16

In I Kings 3:5–15 the choice of Solomon, seeking wisdom rather than gold, is related. God was so pleased with Solomon, He promised him both. You cannot be wise and remain poor; it is almost impossible. Treasures are the by-product of wisdom. But the desire of knowledge and the ability to use knowledge always brings a reward.

Jesus said, "Seek ye first the kingdom of God and His righteousness, and all these things shall be added unto you" (Matthew 6:33). Too many people want wealth without earning it. They do not seek skill, knowledge, or wisdom. If our goal is money, we will not gain it. If our goal is knowledge, wealth and understanding, wealth will surely come.

AN HUMBLE SPIRIT VERSUS A PROUD SPIRIT

Better it is to be of an humble spirit with the lowly, than to divide the spoil with the proud.—Proverbs 16:19

Nothing is more nauseating than pride. A proud person is filled with himself. He cares not for anyone else. His pride detracts from whatever else he may accomplish. He destroys his laurels and rewards.

Great people are humble. Someone asked Hudson Taylor's wife if he were ever tempted to be proud of his accomplishments?

Hudson Taylor frowned and replied, "What accomplishments?" His humility made him great.

QUIETNESS VERSUS STRIFE

Better is a dry morsel, and quietness therewith, than an house full of sacrifices with strife.—Proverbs 17:1

"Do you ever whittle?" Vance Havner asked.

"I haven't heard that word since I was a boy in Georgia," we replied.

"That's just the trouble," he said. "We have forgotten to whittle."

What Havner meant was that people have forgotten to meditate. The Quiet Hour is lost. We should take time to pray. Instead, our life is filled with turmoil and confusion. We should take more time to pray and meditate.

THE POOR VERSUS THE FOOL

Better is the poor that walketh in his integrity, than he that is perverse in his lips, and is a fool.—Proverbs 19:1

One of the greatest naturalists of all time, Thoreau, refused to take a full time job, but did odd jobs, so he could spend his time in the woods studying nature. He cared little for money and lived most simply. He enjoyed living. If you must choose between honesty and wealth which is gained by deception, then choose poverty.

A GOOD NAME VERSUS RICHES

A good name is rather to be chosen than great riches, and loving favour rather than silver and gold.—Proverbs 22:1

Some people can walk into a bank, sign their name, and walk out with thousands of dollars. Others with much wealth cannot do business with anyone. The name makes the difference! If being a Christian does not give you a good name, then you should ask yourself, "Am I really a Christian?"

God Hears Prayer

WHY SOME PRAYERS ARE NOT ANSWERED

The Lord is far from the wicked: but he heareth the prayer of the righteous.—Proverbs 15:29

Our text indicates why many prayers are not answered. An unrighteous person cannot commune with God. The only prayer a sinner can pray is, "God be merciful to me a sinner." God is holy and righteous. He cannot fellowship where there is sin. A sinner cannot reach God, either in worship, prayer or communion. A great barrier exists between him and God.

In the book of Exodus 25:17–22, God told Moses to make a mercy seat of gold to rest upon the ark of the covenant in the holy of holies. There blood was to be sprinkled once a year by the high priest. It was there, where the blood was sprinkled, that God promised, "I will meet with thee, and I will commune with thee." Only when our sins are covered with the blood of Christ are we able to pray to God.

Another reason our prayers are not answered is our carnality in asking. James 4:3 says, we "ask amiss, that we may consume it upon our own lusts." Selfish and carnal prayers are not answered, fortunately.

The psalmist said, "If I regard iniquity in my heart, the Lord will not hear me" (Psalm 66:18). Anyone who is conscious of unforgiven sin has no power in prayer. First, all sin must be confessed and corrected before we can expect to have power with God in prayer. Where there is sin, fellowship is lost.

James 1:6 says, "Let him ask in faith," and it adds as a word of warning to those who lack faith, "Let not that man (who lacks faith) think that he shall receive any thing of the Lord" (James 1:7). Jesus taught us that if we had the faith the size of the grain of mustard seed, we could pray

113

and remove mountains. But many who claim to have faith do not. It is a waste of time to pray if you lack faith.

Then there are those who pray wrongly in that they do not pray in the name of Jesus Christ. Jesus said, "If ye shall ask anything in my name, I will do it" (John 14:14). If you had a check that was signed with the wrong name, would a bank cash it? All of our blessings are in Christ Jesus. We must ask blessings in His name, for it is His name that must be signed to the check of our prayers. "My God shall supply all your need according to his riches in Christ Jesus" (Philippians 4:19). There is only one mediator between God and man, the man Christ Jesus (I Timothy 2:5). If you pray in another name, do not expect to have your prayer answered.

Make sure that you address your prayer to the Father in heaven, and ask in the name of Christ. When the disciples asked the Lord to teach them to pray, He taught them to begin prayer, "Our Father, which art in heaven." The Father is the one who decides what the answer will be. In Romans 8:26, we are informed that the Holy Spirit presents our petitions to the Father for us in a way we cannot. In Romans 8:34, we are reminded that Christ maketh intercession for us. But in Romans 8:32, we are told that it is the Father, who gave the Son, who will also freely give us all things.

When you pray, make sure you pray within the will of God. For God will not answer a request which is contrary to His will, particularly if it is contrary to His expressed will in the Scriptures. Christ Jesus prayed in the Garden of Gethsemane, "Nevertheless, thy will be done." In John 14:" Jesus said, "If ye abide in me, and my words abide in you, ye shall ask what ye will, and it shall be done unto you." God is sovereign. We must ask according to His expressed Word, which Word should abide within us to control our every desire and request.

Make sure that your prayer is unselfish, that it is for the glory of God, that it is righteous in its motive and intent, and that it is for the good of others, God, and His kingdom. Pray Scripturally. The Syrophenician woman who sought the healing of her daughter, came to Jesus on the basis of the Messianic healings of Israel, but she was a Gentile and had no right to this blessing. Christ ignored her. But when she changed her prayer on the basis of His divine grace, He granted her request. (Matthew 15:21–28). Make sure that you pray Scripturally.

GOD HEARS ALL PRAYERS

He heareth the prayer of the righteous.—Proverbs 15: 29

Yes, it is true that God hears all of the prayers of the righteous who pray within His will, Scripturally, and with clean hearts. Did Jesus not say, "Ask and it shall be given you; seek, and ye shall find; knock, and it shall be opened unto you" (Matthew 6:7). He added, that *"every one* that asketh receiveth."

Does God always give us what we ask in the way we wish? No, He does not. But He does hear our prayer, and He does answer according to His will, doing that which is best for us. God hears every prayer and answers, saying either, "Yes," or, "No," or "Wait." Or He may answer our prayer in a much better way, which is best for us. We should commit ourselves into His hands that we will want only His will, which is always best for us.

Read Matthew 18:19. Many times we have claimed this promise and God has never failed. Again, read Matthew 21:22, and claim it. What a marvellous promise! We have proven it over and over again.

GOD DELIVERS THOSE WHO PRAY

For a just man falleth seven times, and riseth up again: but the wicked shall fall into mischief.—Proverbs 24:16

God has not promised that Christians will be immune to trouble. He has frankly warned us that troubles will increase if we live righteously. But the difference between the Christian and the sinner is that the Christian may retreat to prayer, and is always delivered. He falls, but he falls upon his knees! He falls to arise again, for God answers his prayers.

The sinner, too, has troubles, but he falls not to arise again. He is defeated. He cannot pray. He has no source of power and victory.

God Is Sovereign

ALL THINGS ARE MADE BY THE LORD

*The Lord hath made all things for himself: yea, even
the wicked for the day of evil.*—Proverbs 16:4

Our God is a sovereign God. He is above all, and He controls the universe, and all the creatures that dwell therein.
We were made in the image of God; that is, we are intellectual beings, and we are spiritual beings. We have the
power of choice, the power to think, the power to feel, the
power to act. But God is above and over us. Our free-will
agency is a limited sovereignty, limited within the sovereignty
of God. There is nothing God cannot do; man is limited in
capability. God knows all things; man's knowledge is very
small compared to God's omniscience. God is everywhere,
omnipresent; man is limited to his body.

It is extremely important that we recognize our position
within the will of God. Sin is essentially man's rebellion
against the sovereignty of God. But man cannot go beyond
God's permissive will. Man is not all-sufficient. We depend
on God. We must acknowledge God and yield to Him. Even
though we may fight against God, eventually we must bow
to His will in death. Man is but dust.

ALL THINGS ARE MADE BY THE LORD

The Lord hath made all things for himself.—Proverbs
16:4

Man wishes to exalt himself. He would like to think that
he has within himself the powers of creation, denying that
God created man and all things within creation. Man wishes
to ignore God, claiming that creation came by accident, and
that man came by a process of evolution. Man by his intellect, evolutionists would say, improved himself step by step
until he became what he is today. They claim that creation
by evolution is still in process. But God said, after He had

116

created all things including man, that He rested from creation (Genesis 2:1–3).

Nothing came into existence by chance. Creation came by divine choice and design. Creation is too intricate to think it came by accident. There is design and a plan in all creation. Things could not just have happened that perfectly!

Creation proves that God is good, and God is love. He did not have to create the butterflies with their gorgeously colored wings, nor flowers with their beauty and fragrance. Nor did He have to teach the birds to sing. By choice He painted the sky with sunsets and sunrises. He feeds billions of creatures daily, and He has hidden in the earth metals, jewels, chemicals, and all material things which man needs. If man lacks anything, it is not the fault of God. No one need be in want.

We owe all to God. We dwell on His earth. We eat His bread, and drink His water. We build with His trees, and eat His vegetables. We breathe His air. What ingrates we would be to dwell on His earth and then not thank Him. However, some are not only unthankful, they even deny the very existence of God! How inexcusable.

We are answerable to God. He is Creator, and as His creatures, we must expect to answer to God, daily, and then finally at the judgment in the hereafter. God has a right to ask a tithe of us that His gospel might be preached. Whatever we give to Him is already His, but He demands our gifts, so He may bless us with them! What if there were no churches, no preachers of the gospel of His love? We must answer to Him eventually.

We dare not defy God. He is an almighty God, and to defy Him is futile and ridiculous. For in Him we live, move, breathe, and have our very being. He is the Giver of life. He holds our breath in His hands. How foolish it is to disobey or displease Him. How quickly He could snuff out our very life.

We belong to God. He made us; He owns us. A beast recognizes the authority of its master. Do you?

All we own belongs to God. He has but loaned it to us. Nothing is ours, and our prized possession of His creative materials will be given to another who will follow after us.

ALL THINGS ARE MADE FOR THE LORD

The Lord hath made all things for himself.—Proverbs 16:4

God made you for a purpose: for His own glory. Then does He not have a right to expect you to produce? If you made a car, do you not have a right to use it? If you planted a tree and it did not bear fruit, what would you do? What will God do with you if you do not fulfill the purpose for which He created you?

God owns us twice: He made us, and He also bought us with the price of His own blood. Should we not give Him that which rightfully belongs to Him?

When we accept Christ and give our life to God, then we begin to live and fulfill the purpose of life, but until then, our life is squandered. No man enters into the fulfillment of life until he is a Christian.

Without God, life is aimless. But once we are saved, we have someone and something to live for—God. Paul said, "For me to live is Christ."

We were made: (1) to love God, and be loved of God; (2) to worship God; (3) to glorify God with our lives, our words, and our service. Those who live for the flesh dishonor God. Dope, drink, and misuse of sex are fleshly, immoral, and sinful. Idolatry is wrong and unforgiveable, and we are idolators whenever we worship anything but our Creator. Worship of material things, pleasure, sex—all these are idolatry!

COMMIT THYSELF UNTO THE LORD

Commit thy works unto the Lord, and thy thoughts shall be established. When a man's ways please the Lord, he maketh even his enemies to be at peace with him. A man's heart deviseth his way: but the Lord directeth his steps.—Proverbs 16:3, 7, 9

To commit yourself to God is the same as to believe in the Lord Jesus Christ. Commit yourself to Christ for salvation, eternal life, forgiveness of sins, and heaven. Jesus never fails!

The Christ-centered life is a successful life. It is a rewarding life. It is a happy and joyful life. It is life with purpose and objective. Christ came that we might have the more abundant life (John 10:10).

God has a blueprint for every life (Romans 4:29; 12:1, 2; I Thessalonians 5:18). Turn your life over to God, and He will fulfill His plan and purpose for you. Then, and only then, will you get the most out of your life.

Self Mastery

PRIDE BRINGS DESTRUCTION

Pride goeth before destruction, and an haughty spirit before a fall. Better it is to be of an humble spirit with the lowly, than to divide the spoil with the proud.
—Proverbs 16:18–19

The human race has mastered land, ocean, and now the skies. We have mastered the power of steam, oil, and now nuclear power. We have mastered the chemistry of the body, and natural sciences. We have mastered the animal world and the electricity in the sky. We know how to send sound and pictures through the air without wires. We have advanced to the point where we could even destroy the entire planet with one cobalt bomb the size of a basketball!* But few man have mastered themselves! They are slaves to passion, lust, and hate. They are slaves to dope, drink, and sex lusts. They cannot conquer social evils: war, slavery, poverty Not until man is able to conquer himself will he be the master of all things. God made us to be free, not slaves.

Edith Torrey once said to her father, Dr. R. A. Torrey "Father, at last I have arrived at the place where I have complete control of my temper."

"Yes, Edith, I have noticed that," Dr. Torrey said. "But am praying, Edith, that the time will come when you are so completely filled with the love of Christ, you will not have a temper to control."

Not until we realize such victory will we be masters of ourselves (Proverbs 16:32; 25:28).

Pride is the basis of all sin. When Satan tempted Adam and Eve, it was on the basis of pride. He invited them to eat the forbidden fruit that they might be wise and become a

* The Author was briefed as to this fact, Washington, D.C. in a secret meeting of national Religious Broadcasters by a government representative.

gods. Most sin today is communal sin: "Keeping up with the
Joneses!" We wish to be well thought of. We yearn for
human acclaim and recognition, and will do anything required to achieve it. We fear getting out of step with the
common customs. "All we like sheep have gone astray"
(Isaiah 53:6). Most of our sins are social sins which we
share together. We drink, and we smoke, because it is the
custom of our day. Now it is social among youth to use
dope, regardless of its consequences and dangers. Sinners are
afraid to use their own reason, and they obey the voice of
man rather than the voice of God.

How much better it would be if we had enough humility
to stop caring what others think or say, and care only to
please God. Humility would save us from sin. But people
burn with pride. Pride is actually love of self, and it is most
repulsive.

Pride produces the sin of anger. Orientals say, "I must
save my face." So must we all! But until you master your
anger, you are a weakling. A strong character controls temper. Some are even proud of their temper! They should be
ashamed of their lack of self-control. Some people proudly
boast, "I have a mean temper. It is the German in me," or
else they blame it on some other ethnic background. The
truth is, it is the devil in them!

Pride produces jealousy within you. This is another of the
common sins of the spirit that spawn from the eggs of pride.
We would not be jealous of others if we were not proud and
anxious to put self above all others. Let's conquer this sin
and master self. Jealousy is like a cancer in the soul, and it
is as dangerous as smallpox.

Pride is also the father of greed. Nothing gnaws into the
soul of man like greed. *Covetousness* is the twin brother of
greed. They were born together. These sins of the soul lead
to the worship of materialism. Jesus said much about materialism as a false god. (Matthew 6:19–34; Luke 12:15–
34).

Pride breeds hate against those you *envy*. If mental sickness were understood as well as physical sickness, hatred
would be on a par with cancer—just as dangerous and just
as far reaching, resulting in death.

Become the master of your own mind and soul. Conquer
these spiritual sicknesses. You must recognize them and desire to overcome them. You alone can do this.

Trust in the Lord Brings Joy

He that handleth a matter wisely shall find good: and whoso trusteth in the Lord, happy is he.—Proverbs 16:20

The shortest route to self-mastery is trust in the Lord. We trust in the Lord for salvation. But we also trust the Lord for much more. To trust is to believe in, to yield to, to commit your all to God.

Trust in the Lord, then, is the secret of rest and peace of mind. We no longer strive or fight against circumstances when we trust in the Lord. Once you completely yield yourself to God, you cease to row against the waves and storm of circumstances. You accept His will as best for you and rest in Him. This is peace!

Trust is the cure for worry. Worry never changes anything, nor does it accomplish anything. Commit your way unto the Lord and He will bring it to pass. How much better it is to trust God than to fight for human glory.

Trust is the chair of contentment. Paul wrote, "I have learned in whatsoever state I am, therewith to be content." Again he said, "Contentment is great gain" (I Timothy 6:6).

Trust is the secret of courage. What have we to fear when we trust God? He will keep that which we have committed unto Him.

Trust is also the key to success. Restless, greedy, proud people never win friends, and they lose business. Life to them is filled with trouble.

Understanding Is a Wellspring of Life

Understanding is a wellspring of life unto him that hath it: but the instruction of fools is folly.—Proverbs 16:22

In contrast with pride and conflict is understanding. If only people understood each other, there would be no wars, no racial conflicts, no personality conflicts. This, then, is the basis of all human relationships, and is therefore the very wellspring of life. From this well we draw successful living.

Understanding is the basis for human sympathy. If we only knew the cross our brother bears, we would care.

Understanding is the basis for peace. To see from another's viewpoint is to become involved in his problems. This

eads to peace and lending assistance. It replaces condem-
ation and hate.

Understanding is the basis of patience. We will endure
nother's faults if we understand their cause.

The Hour of Temptation

TEMPTATION IS FOR REFINING

The fining pot is for silver, and the furnace for gold: but the Lord trieth the hearts. Take away the dross from the silver, and there shall come forth a vessel for the finer.—Proverbs 17:3; 25:4

The word temptation in the Bible means literally, testing. We read in Matthew 4:1 that the Holy Spirit led Jesus into the wilderness to be tempted. This is a strange statement. Why would the Spirit of God lead the Son, Jesus Christ, to be tempted? It is our objective to discover the answer. We may be sure that there is a good reason for temptation.

On the other hand, James 1:13 states that God never tempts any man. God may lead us into the place of temptation, but He never tempts us. Satan does that. However, God allows us to be tempted only for our own good. And Satan can never tempt us without the permission of God. When Satan appeared before the Lord in heaven, he had his eyes on Job but confessed he could not touch him unless the Lord permitted it. God had built a hedge about Job. He protects us also.

We have one assuring promise, God will not permit us to be tempted beyond that which we can stand, and He always provides a way of escape (I Corinthians 10:13). Paul rejoiced in his temptations (II Corinthians 12:7–10).

Temptation is for the purpose of making us Christlike. A silversmith watched as silver ore was being refined in the hot furnace fire, and he did not remove the ore as long as the smoke burned from the ore. An onlooker became greatly disturbed and cried, "You will burn up the ore. Take it out of the fire!"

The silversmith was unperturbed and left the ore in the intense fires of refining, until he could see his face reflected

124

in the ore. Then he cried out, "Take the ore out of the fire!" Then he explained to the onlooker, "You see, the fire never burns up the ore, only the dross. I know when the dross is all burned out when I can see my face in the ore."

So it is with the Christian in the fires of trial. God allows us to be tried until He can see the beauty of His face reflected in us.

Fires of trial only refine us, never burn us. When the three Hebrew children were cast into the fiery furnace, the intense fires only burned the thongs that bound them! Jesus said to Peter, "Satan hath desired thee to sift thee as wheat, but I have prayed for thee." All Satan could do was to sift the chaff from Peter. So it is with you.

Refining is to make us fit for service. A vessel cannot be used until it is cleansed and purified. Refining makes us fit for the Master's use (II Timothy 2:20,21).

A Christian lives to bear fruit. His purpose on earth is fruit bearing, but no Christian is capable of bearing fruit until he is cleansed and purged from sin. We must be pruned, and the runners must be cut off of the vine and burned before we are brought close enough to the root to be fruitful (John 15:2).

Trials strengthen us. We grow strong through testings just as muscles of an athlete grow strong by fighting against an enemy. If we never had trials, we would become spiritual weaklings. Trees grow strong through the buffeting of the winds, the burning of hot suns, and the thirst of drought. Through storms it roots deep and reaches for the hidden streams of water. So it is with the Christian (Psalm 1).

TEMPTATION REVEALS TRUE FRIENDS

A friend loveth at all times, and a brother is born for adversity.—Proverbs 17:17

We have many friends until trouble comes knocking at our door. Then we discover who is really our friend. Fair weather friends are worse than useless. The person who still loves you when you lose your job, your money, your reputation, and your health is a true friend.

Christ Jesus is a friend that sticketh closer than a brother. Some years ago, two brothers in New England became involved in a bank holdup. A gunman they hired shot and killed a teller, contrary to their plans and wishes. But they died in an electric chair.

The entire community hated them and despised them, with one exception—their mother. She stood over the pine box in the grave and bathed it with her tears. She still held them in her arms and nursed them in her imagination. They were her boys, her former babies. No matter what they had done, she still loved them.

In the hour of testing and trial, God still loves you. Though you may stumble and fall, He still loves you. It takes temptation to reveal God's love.

Furthermore, you will never really get acquainted with God, His might and power, His goodness and forgiveness, until you go through the deep waters and floods. The fires of trial and hate will not burn you. God did not promise you would not go through testings; He frankly told you that you would! He foretold testings. It is then that He goes with you, and will never leave you nor forsake you (Isaiah 43:2). Did you ask to know Him, as Paul did? (Philippians 3:10). He walks with you in trouble, and you get to know Him. Did you ask for more faith? Faith comes through trials.

God led Israel into the wilderness and there he tried them with thirst, hunger, and fiery serpents. In the hour of trouble, they learned their need of God, and their weaknesses of the flesh were revealed. Trial taught them to seek God's cleansing power and taught them to rely on God.

THE LORD IS OUR REFUGE IN TEMPTATION

The name of the Lord is a strong tower: the righteous runneth into it, and is safe.—Proverbs 18:10

Temptation drives us to God, not from God. When Don LeTourneau was suddenly and tragically killed in his plane, we remarked, "I hope this does not discourage Bob in the good he is doing for the Lord."

A friend replied, "Trials don't drive men from God, but to God. This will but refine Bob and make him an even better Christian." And it did!

Nothing can harm the Christian. No matter what weapon or enemy is raised up against you, it cannot harm you, for your life is hid in God, in Christ Jesus. God has promised it will not hurt you (Isaiah 54:17).

Trials will but strengthen your faith. The more you are tried, the more God will defend you. Your faith will grow strong under temptation.

Avoid Alcoholic Beverages

WINE IS A MOCKER

Wine is a mocker, strong drink is raging: and whosoever is deceived thereby is not wise.—Proverbs 20:1

In the Old Testament, the original Hebrew carefully designates all drinks the same as in the English, such as beer, wine, whiskey, and ale. But in the New Testament, the Greek language does not distinguish between beverages. The Greek word *oinos* means literally *fruit juice*. Whether or not the juice has alcoholic content is designated by the added adjectives *new* or *old* wine. New wine is non-intoxicating, and old wine is alcoholic.

When Paul wrote to Timothy to drink a "little wine for thy stomach's sake and thine often infirmities," the wine was fruit juice.

When Christ changed water to wine, again the word is fruit juice. It had no time to ferment. The wine used in communion symbolizes the blood of Christ, and Christ was without sin. But fermentation is always a type of sin. Therefore the wine of communion had to be without fermentation, otherwise it would indicate that Christ's blood was sinful, and that He was a sinner.

Wine is a mocker in the sense that it is a false stimulant. Alcohol does not stimulate, it merely deadens the portion of the brain which warns against fatigue, giving a person a false sense of security, which may lead him to overdo.

Strong drink is raging in the sense that it leads to quarreling and fighting. Did you ever notice that many murders are committed in saloons? Most of the police cases emanate from drink. One police agency informed us that more than 90 percent of all auto accidents in our area were caused by drink. How foolish, then, it is for one to drink wine!

How true is our text: "Whosoever is deceived thereby is

not wise." Many drink so they will be keen and astute mentally, but drink destroys the powers of the intellect. As Christians, we have given our bodies and our all to Christ, to serve Him. Shall we destroy our powers to think and to serve Him with drink?

DRINK BRINGS SORROW

Who hath woe? who hath sorrow? who hath contentions? who hath babbling? who hath wounds without cause? who hath redness of eyes? They that tarry long at the wine; they that go to seek mixed wine.—Proverbs 23:29, 30

Read Proverbs 21:17, and 23:29–35. Some would argue that there is no Scripture in the Bible against the use of alcoholic beverages. This is not so.

The most forceful tool of argument is a question, for it forces people to think. The writer resorts to this powerful tool of the question and asks questions which all should carefully consider and answer.

First, who is it who has endless sorrow and woe? Men drink to drown their sorrows, but drink brings sorrow. As a former chaplain at a federal penitentiary, I can testify to the fact that many of the men behind the bars were there because of deeds committed while under the influence of intoxicants. Crimes committed under the influence of drink would never have been done under normal circumstances.

Secondly, who is always quarreling? It is the person who drinks. He is in a constant brawl! He is a problem to his family, to the police, and to himself. Our jails would be almost empty if it were not for drink. Drinking costs the tax payers billions of dollars each year.

Who is always wounded and bleeding? The man who drinks! He often appears in bandages. And he finally dies with delirium tremens, or internally bleeds to death with sclerosis of the liver. How foolish to go to an untimely grave through drink.

Who becomes poverty stricken and comes to want? Who is it that walks Skid Row, and goes to the missions without a friend? It is the man who drinks (Proverbs 21:17).

A Fort Wayne, Indiana, man went to Detroit on business. He went to a tavern for a drink. When he saw the

people who were in the tavern he suddenly realized that the
were all poverty stricken and failures. He left the taver
without his drink, came to church the next Sunday and ac
cepted Christ as his Saviour. "I saw what drink was leadin
me to, so I have come to Christ for deliverance," he sai

The wine may sparkle, but in the end it stings like a
adder. In Europe there is a wine cup which is used when
person is drinking too much. In the bottom of the cup is
serpent with ruby eyes. The drinker comes to the bottor
of the cup, sees the serpent, drops the cup and flees from
the tavern. All should see the serpent in the cup, not just
few who are overdrinking!

Proverbs 23:33 indicates the sickness alcohol causes—
delirium tremens, hardening of the arteries and liver. Th
victim sees false and frightening visions and fear grips hi
heart.

Proverbs 23:34-35 describes the mental numbness tha
drink brings, so that a person staggers like a sailor at sea
and cannot walk normally. He doesn't feel his injuries. Bu
he returns for more drink afterward, for he becomes a slave
to his appetitie. Before you drink, consider these things

DRINK DESTROYS MORALITY

(Proverbs 31:3-7)

*It is not for kings, O Lemuel, it is not for kings to
drink wine; nor for princes strong drink: Lest they
drink, and forget the law, and pervert the judgment
of any of the afflicted.*—Proverbs 31:4, 5

Drink is not for kings, for it destroys moral judgment
Many a nation has been destroyed and given away by ruler
who have gathered about peace tables under the influence o
liquor. A judge at a bench, if drinking, would not give fai
judgment. Political corruption results from drink.

France fell before the guns of Germany, until the Ger
mans reached the wine cellars of France during Worl
War I. The wine was their conqueror.

If drink destroys moral balance for kings, it does so fo
Christians also. If we are to follow Christ, we cannot do so
under the influence of drink. God's Word commands, "B
not drunk with wine" (Ephesians 5:18). The Holy Spirit i
the source of our strength, not wine.

Wine can be used only for medicine, and for psychiatric treatment according to Proverbs 31:6,7. However, alcohol has many evil side effects when used medically, and today we have other medicines so far superior without the bad side effects, that it is no longer considered a good medicine.

Man's Dependence Upon God

MAN CANNOT SAVE HIMSELF

Who can say, I have made my heart clean, I am pure from my sin?—Proverbs 20:9

Man is always seeking salvation that glorifies himse rather than the Son of God, the Saviour. Man wants to b able to boast of what he has done. Therefore he seeks sa vation on the basis of his own merit. He resents an invita tion that beckons him to come forward to make a publi confession of his faith in Christ. He avoids kneeling at th altar of prayer, confessing his sins. He tries to escape re pentance. He goes so far as to deny that he is guilty and sinner, or even needs a Saviour.

Jesus made it clear: "Except ye repent, ye shall likewis perish."

Men shun the blood-stained way of Calvary as the way t heaven, but the Scriptures warn, "Without the shedding c blood there is no remission (forgiveness) (Hebrews 9:22. God is a just God, and sin must be punished. God canno forgive sin because we are sorry. Sin must be paid for befor it can be forgiven.

Men want to be saved by their own good works, bu Ephesians 2:8–10 says, "For by grace are ye saved, throug faith; and that not of yourselves: it is the gift of God: no of works, lest any man should boast. For we are his worl manship, created in Christ Jesus unto good works, whic God hath before ordained that we should walk therein Titus 3:5 states clearly, "Not by works of righteousnes which ye have done, but according to his mercy he saved u by the washing of regeneration, and renewing of the Hol Ghost; which He shed on us abundantly through Christ o Saviour."

We are not saved by what we do, but by the Saviour an what He did on the cross for us. But as surely as we ar saved, we will do what is pleasing to God and is right.

Some would save themselves by ritual and baptism, but Galatians 6:15 says that baptism and ritual do not save us, but we are saved through a new creation, or new birth. Salvation is by regeneration, not reformation.

Man seeks to rid himself of guilt through a psychiatrist, but Christ alone can remove guilt. Nothing short of the blood of Christ can relieve man of a sense of guilt.* It is shocking that the highest percentage of suicides among professions is that of the psychiatrists, who cannot remove either their guilt, or yours.

MAN CANNOT AVENGE HIMSELF

Say not thou, I will recompense evil; but wait on the Lord, and he shall save thee.—Proverbs 20:22

The man without Christ lives by the law of the jungle. He rewards those who show him good with good, and he also seeks vengeance against those who deal falsely with him. We call it politics, and all people are natural politicians. But Christ taught us to live by the law of love. He told us to love our enemies. To do good to those who do evil to us. We are to walk the second mile for our enemies (Matthew 5:38–48).

Vengeance always makes the perpetrator of "getting even" as wicked as the person who first did the wrong against you. We are not to be overcome with evil, but to overcome evil with good.

Those who seek vengeance fail to show love, which is the motivating principle of the Christian.

We are told what we are to do in reply to evil: show kindness in return (Romans 12:17–21).

The Christian is to live by the Golden Rule: "Do unto others as you would have them do unto you." How can you fulfill this law of love and still seek vengeance?

An evil deed against you is but an opportunity for you to demonstrate the love of God and your Christianity. Turn your enemy's evil deed into an opportunity to demonstrate what it means to be a Christian and try to win your enemy to Christ.

* Janet Chusmir, Knight Newspaper Writer, Elyria, Ohio; Chronicle Telegram, p. 3, July 31, 1973

MAN CANNOT GUIDE HIMSELF

Man's goings are of the Lord; how can a man then understand his own way?—Proverbs 20:24

Wouldn't it be wonderful if we were able to know the future? We could plan and design our lives and always make the right choice. But no man knows the future. We cannot know what will happen in politics, finance, weather, or in any other thing. We may guess, and try to profit by past events, but there are always peculiar and new influences which alter the course of events. So we can never know what really will happen.

But the Christian has dwelling within his heart one who does know the future: Christ dwells in him. God has the power to foretell, for He is omniscient. How wonderful it is to be able to turn your life over to the Lord and permit Him to guide you with His eye. Prayer opens the gate into the future for you. God will lead you and direct your path. The Christian has a great advantage over the man of the world.

MAN CANNOT DEFEND HIMSELF

The horse is prepared against the day of battle: but safety is of the Lord.—Proverbs 21:31

We may arm ourselves with planes, tanks, guns, and even atomic bombs, but we can never be sure of what our enemies may do.

David numbered his forces, and God punished him. How could David know the number of angels fighting for him? How could he know what his forces actually were? If he had trusted in the Lord, the Lord would have defended him. "If God be for you, who can be against you?"

Satan may make sundry attacks against you, but God is your defender and keeper. You are the apple of His eye.

When the Syrians lay siege to Israel, God drove them out through their own imaginations (II Kings 7:1–15). When Sennacherib attacked Hezekiah, and scorned God, God smote 185,000 of the Syrian army with disease and defeated them (II Kings 19:35). God is your defender, and your strong tower of defense. Trust in the Lord, and He will fight for you.

Oppress Not the Poor

OPPRESS NOT THE POOR MAN

(Proverbs 19:17, 22:16; 22:23; 29:7)

Rob not the poor, because his poor: neither oppress the afflicted in the gate: for the Lord will plead their cause, and spoil the soul of those that spoiled them.— Proverbs 22:22–23

So few Christians ever stop to think about the poor. We seem totally unconscious of our moral obligation for the poor. And yet, there is nothing that tests the soul of a man more than poverty and need. At such a time, he may hunger, or need clothing, or medicine, and if other Christians do not care, he may secretly condemn them for their hardness of heart and lack of love.

When Christ fed the five thousand, He looked upon them with compassion, because they had no food. He knew they would faint by the wayside as they journeyed home if they were not fed. Do we notice the need of others? If not, can we say that we have the spirit of Christ? God does care for the poor and needy; let us not give them the impression that we do not care, causing them to think that God does not care.

Proverbs has much to say about oppressing the poor. Let us examine a few of these passages.

In Proverbs 19:17 God considers that whatever you give to help the poor is a loan to Him, and He will repay you in behalf of the poor with interest. You cannot outgive God! He will be no man's debtor. God's credit is always good, and He will repay. So be sure that when you give to the poor, God will give it back to you. He said He would.

Proverbs 22:16 warns that some even tread upon the poor, taking advantage of them, in order to increase their own riches! Such a person will come to want. God promises that he will. God will not bless such a person. James 2:15,

135

16 warns of impending judgment upon such. Proverbs 22:22, 23 is almost a repetition of James 5:1–6.

Proverbs 29:7 says if a person is truly a Christian, he will not tread upon the poor, but he will help him. Unsaved men often have no compunction of conscience regarding the poor. James says caring for the fatherless and widows in their affliction is true religion (James 1:27).

DESPISE NOT THE POOR

The poor is hated even of his own neighbor: but the rich hath many friends . . . Whoso mocketh the poor reproacheth his Maker: and he that is glad at calamities shall not be unpunished . . . Love not sleep, lest thou come to poverty; open thine eyes, and thou shalt be satisfied with bread.—Proverbs 14:20; 17:5; 21:13

It is not true that clothes make the man. And it is not true that the rich are the best people in the world. We must learn to consider a man on the basis of his character, his morality, his kindness, his graciousness.

James warns against giving the rich the best seats in the synagogue or church. He reminds us that some rich people oppress the poor, and some are not good Christians (James 2:1–9). Some of the godliest of people are poor.

Spurgeon once said, "If you would fill your church with the wealthy and rich, bring into the church the poor, for some day they will be rich."

The car a person drives or his bank account does not make him any better than the poor man. Sometimes circumstances defeat a capable person. Others are so occupied doing good, they do not know how to make money. A rich person should be given no better position or have more authority or recognition than a poor man in the church.

Proverbs 17:5 tells us that God says that whosoever mocks the poor is a reproach to his Maker. God is concerned for the poor and needy. God has sufficient food and clothing for all men, and if they are in want, it is man's fault, not God's.

Proverbs 21:13 states that those who refuse to hear the cry of the poor will some day have the taste of poverty. A wealthy actor took a hungry man into a restaurant and bought him a steak dinner. Someone asked him, "Why did you do that?"

He replied, "Because some day I may be hungry and he may be wealthy. Then he will buy me a steak dinner."

Jesus taught that the day would come when He would reward those who fed the poor sheep, but He would punish those who oppressed them (Matthew 25:34-40).

POVERTY CAN BE BETTER THAN RICHES!

(Proverbs 15:16; 16:16; 19:1; 22:1; 28:6)

Better is the poor that walketh in his uprightness, than he that is perverse in his ways, though he be rich.— Proverbs 28:6

Proverbs 15:16—Down through the ages, many of God's saints have suffered poverty because they stood true to Christ. They could have accumulated wealth if they had been willing to sacrifice their principles of righteousness, but they would not. Others have given up an opportunity to earn money, to devote their talents to the Lord's work. In such cases, poverty is better than riches, for the poor are rich in heaven if such be the case.

Proverbs 16:16—Some spend all of their time making money; others spend their time searching out the wisdom of the ages. Those who devote their time to searching out the mind of God in divine revelation, in the Bible, are wealthy with truth, thought, and wisdom. Some of the wisest of men have been the poorest of men. Shall we classify them as poor men?

It is better to be honest, dependable, and trustworthy than it is to sacrifice principle and make wealth. John Bunyan spent twelve years in prison, though a wife and blind daughter were dependent upon him, because he dared to preach of the second coming of Christ. During his imprisonment, he wrote *Pilgrim's Progress* and made the world rich with this great treasure of literature. He himself died a poor man, but was he not rich?

Proverbs 22:1, 2—Years ago in Chicago, I saw a man who was worth more than 100 million dollars walk into church with his chauffeur to the front seat, and the two sat down and worshipped together. Both were Christians, and both were equal before God.

A good name is worth more than treasure. Some wealthy men cannot be trusted, but some poor men have a name that is worth more than gold. They borrow on their signature.

Proverbs 28:6—To be able to walk uprightly, knowing that you have done no wrong, is worth more than a billion dollars. Many a rich man who is perverse in his ways has neither peace nor joy. Trouble and guilt dog his steps, and his wealth does not bring him happiness.

Shun Falsehood and Dishonesty

A FALSE BALANCE

(Proverbs 11:1; 16:11; 20:10; 29:27)

A false balance is abomination to the Lord: but a just weight is his delight . . . An unjust man is an abomination to the just: and he that is upright in the way is abomination to the wicked.—Proverbs 11:1; 29:27

A salesman came forward one Sunday night and accepted Christ as his personal Saviour. The next day he called at the parsonage and attempted to sell "two suits for the price of one!" The minister refused to buy. Before the salesman left, he requested the minister to baptize him the following Sunday and to receive him into the church membership.

"I'm sorry," the minister said, "but I cannot baptize you, nor will I present your name to the church for membership."

"Why not?" the salesman asked in amazement.

"As long as you are selling two suits for the price of one, I cannot baptize you," the minister said. "When you become honest enough to tell the truth—that you are selling two cheap suits for the price of one good suit—then I will be most happy to baptize you. The salesman admitted his sales pitch was dishonest, but it was what his company had taught him to say.

"Dishonesty," the minister said, "is the mark of carnality, and baptism is a public declaration of the new life in Christ. Dishonesty and baptism are incompatible."

Too many Christians are hurting their testimony with a false balance. If your new nature does not make you honest, then there is doubt that you have truly been converted.

A minister traded his car on a new car, and it had a cracked engine head. The dealer had given him the rock-bottom price on the new car because he was a minister. The dealer later said, "I am disillusioned by that minister. I was

thinking of accepting Christ as my Saviour, but he has con
vinced me that Christianity is a sham." The minister had
thought that he was a shrewd trader, but actually, he was
only dishonest.

A LYING TONGUE

(Proverbs 11:9; 12:17–22; 13:5; 14:5; 17:4; 18:6–8;
19:5, 9; 24:28; 25:18; 26:22–28)

*The lip of truth shall be established forever: but a lying
tongue is but for a moment.*—Proverbs 12:19

James said that the mastery of the tongue was the pin
nacle of accomplishment, and it was the mark of spirituality
He devoted an entire chapter to the tongue (James 3).

A lying tongue is the result of a dishonest heart. If a
man's heart is filled with deception, and if he is a hypocrite
then he will lie. That is why some people find it easier to li
than to tell the truth.

A little boy asked his father, who was pastor of the
church, when they were eating their Sunday dinner, "Father
was that story you told this morning true or was it just a
pulpit story?" How careful we must be to always tell the
truth. If anyone should be truthful, it is the Christian. Do
people believe what you say?

The tongue is not only capable of lying, it is also
capable of false witness and gossiping. Jesus said that men
would give an account to God for every idle word. The
word "idle" is literally "gossipy." Many a good character has
been crucified or ruined by a villainous tongue. A false wit
ness was worthy of death under the Old Testament law
Gossiping is a most heinous sin.

A woman came to Dwight L. Moody and confessed, "I
cannot help lying. What shall I do to overcome this terribl
habit?"

Said Moody, "That is a sin of the flesh. The only way to
conquer the flesh is to embarrass it. So every time you
tell a falsehood, immediately confess you have lied and admit
your guilt." She followed his advice and overcame her be
setting sin—lying.

DECEIT

(Proverbs 12:20; 15:8; 17:7, 20; 20:17)

Misrepresentation is so common because the heart of man is filled with deceit. Placing large potatoes on the top of a basket of small potatoes has ruined the testimony of many a Christian. To deceive a person is to insult him. Do not think that people do not see through deception; they are not fools.

Deception reaches its lowest ebb in the field of religion. Those who attempt to cover up their sins with false worship deceive only themselves. God sees through them, and you may be sure others do also.

Deception may bring momentary satisfaction, but in the end his mouth will be as if he had eaten sand!

Don't Be a Glutton

DON'T OVEREAT

*When thou sittest to eat with a ruler, consider diligently
what is before thee: and put a knife to thy throat, if thou
be a man given to appetite.*—Proverbs 23:1, 2

A person who does not control his appetite has no will
power to resist other temptations. We should seek above all
else self-mastery.

A minister refused to overeat when he was being entertained by a person who was well known for her delectable
food. His hostess reproached him, intimating that he did not
appreciate her cuisine, which she had worked so hard to
prepare.

He explained to her, "I have a brother who weighs more
than 350 pounds, and if I overeat, I will gain weight very
fast. I believe this would hinder my testimony in the pulpit,
and I have given my life to serve the Lord. If I do not
demonstrate that God gives me control of my appetite, how
can I possibly tell men that Christ can set them free from
other passions of the flesh?"

What we eat determines our health. Overeating can cause
disease and early death. High blood pressure, diabetes, kidney
trouble, and circulatory disease are affected by obesity.
Every pound of overweight requires extra labor for the
heart.

Our bodies are the temple of the Holy Spirit. It is just as
wrong to overeat as it is to smoke or drink. As a Christian
you owe it to God and yourself not to overindulge in anything.

Proper eating, drinking enough water (at least eight
glasses a day), proper rest, and exercise are the secrets of
good health, a clear mind, and a long life. Good health produces a fuller life; Christianity is practical. Jesus came that
we might enjoy "the more abundant life."

Don't Be Bought With Food

(Proverbs 23:5–8)

Eat thou not the bread of him that hath an evil eye, neither desire thou his dainty meats.—Proverbs 23:6

It is customary in business today to invite a prospective customer to dinner, and thus to win his favor, but more than that, to obligate him. We should be careful to weigh all business decisions. Do not allow food to impair your mental vision. The heart of a man is more important that the food he buys you. For as his heart is, so is he.

Do not allow yourself to be obligated to sinners. Associate with good people and avoid evil people, even if they offer you an abundance of reward.

We are warned, "Labor not to be rich: cease from thine own wisdom." If the objective of your service is money, then you will fail in your designs. If your goal is to help others, to serve God, and to exalt Christ, then God will give you wealth. Did He not promise this to Solomon? Solomon sought wisdom, not wealth, but God gave him both, for you cannot be wise and poor!

Avoid the schemer, though he may try to buy you with food. Choose carefully your companions. Your associations will determine your course in life. Wrong companions will bring you to ruin. Good companions will become your most valuable asset in life.

Gluttony Brings Poverty

Be not among winebibbers; among riotous eaters of flesh: for the drunkard and the glutton shall come to poverty: and drowsiness shall clothe a man with rags.—Proverbs 23:20, 21

Winebibbers and gluttons are not good company. You must do as they do if you make them companions, or else you will not be wanted. To be accepted by drinking men, you must drink. If you are to be one with the glutton, you must eat at his table as he eats.

A visit to any tavern will reveal what drink and gluttony will lead to. Listen to the idle, incoherent talk, see the rags of poverty with which gluttons are clothed, observe how aimless, empty, and useless their lives are, and you will shun their way of life.

You cannot walk with Jesus and the glutton at the same time.

Give Your Heart to God

AS A MAN THINKETH SO IS HE

For as he thinketh in his heart, so is he: Eat and drink, saith he to thee; but his heart is not with thee.—Proverbs 23:7

How important it is that we read only clean and pure literature. If we read hunting magazines, we will wish to go hunting. If we read business magazines, we will become infatuated with business. If we read health-culture magazines, we will become interested in exercise. If we read sex magazines, we will feed the lusts of the flesh, and immorality is apt to result. If we read daily newspapers, we will worry and fret. If we read the Bible, we will find peace and contentment, and our minds will be purified.

It is also important what we see. Television is a training school in crime and cruelty. Beware what you see for the eye is the gate to the heart.

Old Testament law forbade the eating of unclean foods such as animals that did not have cloven hoofs and did not chew the cud. This was but a type of the spiritual and soul food of the Christian. Christ is the Bread of Life. He is the honey in the rock. Whosoever eateth of His flesh and drinketh of His blood will never hunger or thirst.

Philippians 4:8, 9 urges us to think on good things, not evil. There are so many billions of books in the world, why waste time feeding your mind and soul on trash. You will not live long enough to digest all of the treasures of truth in print. So make a covenant with the Lord to read only that which is constructive and good.

A person said, "I am studying all of the error and false religions of the world, so I will be able to answer them."

We replied, "Don't waste your time studying error. Study truth and then you will recognize error when you see it, and you will be able to answer it. Besides, your soul will grow strong on truth; it will starve on error."

What would you do if a thief came into your house a
midnight? Would you shoot him? You would automaticall
do whatever your heart has previously decided is right. Thi
illustrates the importance of your thoughts. The heart is th
mainspring of action. What a man thinketh in his heart so i
he.

The fool hath said in his *heart* there is no God (Psalr
14:1). The infidel's trouble is not in his head, but in hi
heart. His heart is not right with God. It is sinful and evi
Make sure your heart is right.

GIVE YOUR HEART TO GOD

*My son, give me thine heart, and let thine eyes observe
my ways.*—Proverbs 23:26

Men are ever trying to change the evil actions of men b
improving their environment. They seek through reforn
education, and good environment to make men better. Th
is like putting a poultice on a boil when the blood stream
corrupt and needs cleansing.

It is said that the leopard is the one animal that cannot b
tamed. But a leopard can be changed if he were given a ne
heart. This is exactly what God does for sinful man. H
changes the heart of man (Ezekiel 36:26, 27).

David said, "Thy Word have I hid in my heart, that
might not sin against thee." The cure for all sin is a chang
of heart. New housing is good, but it is not the answer to ou
troubles. The gospel alone offers to change the hearts of mer

"My son, give thy heart," God says. To do this we mu
invite Christ into our hearts, to take complete possession o
our mind, our soul, and our affections. Let Him rul
supreme in your life. Then alone will you find victory ove
sin and temptation. The heart is the center of our affection
The rich ruler was willing to follow Jesus, but he was no
willing to give up his wealth to follow Jesus. His heart wa
given to his money, and not to God. Christ summed up th
commandments thus, "Love the Lord with all thy heart."

OUT OF THE HEART ARE THE ISSUES OF LIFE

*Keep thy heart with all diligence; for out of it are the
issues of life.*—Proverbs 4:23

Jesus said that all sin is hatched in the heart of man Matthew 15:18–20). Men's hearts He described as a cockaice den, with eggs of evil that hatch out into sin.

We should guard our hearts as we would guard diamonds nd gold. Set a watch upon your heart. Keep evil out!

The Parable of the Neglected Field

EVIL THRIVES THROUGH NEGLECT

*I went by the field of the slothful, and by the vineyard
of the man void of understanding; and, lo, it was all
grown over with thorns, and nettles had covered the
face thereof, and the stone wall thereof was broken
down.*—Proverbs 24:30, 31

Personally, I make a very poor gardener. Not because
am lazy and neglect my garden, but because I am so busy
and am away so often, the weeds get ahead of me. Soon
the spinach, the carrots, the beets and other garden vegetables are lost among the weeds and choked out.

I once visited a farm in eastern Ohio, which had been
without an occupant for more than three years. It had been
one of the most productive farms in the area. The soil was
excellent, and the buildings superb, but in three years weeds
had overtaken the farm. They were shoulder high. The
hinges on the barn doors were rusting, and the building
needed paint. Windows of the house were broken, and wild
animals and birds had taken over the yard. Rats had bur-
rowed under the buildings, and worms infested the fruit.
Fruit trees were bleeding from pests. I thought of our
parable.

The writer of Proverbs said he saw this, and he also considered it well. He took instruction from the parable. First, let
us learn the lesson that evil needs no encouragement. It
thrives and prospers through neglect. A nation that neglects worship and spiritual life will soon come to ruin. The
home that neglects the family altar will soon end in divorce
and the children will go astray. A life that neglects personal
devotions, church, Bible study, and prayer will soon be over
run with evil habits and sin.

Communism thrives and prospers where there is spiritual
neglect. The use of dope and narcotics never bothers the

spiritual person who is taught the Word of God. Those who have been raised without God are the victims of such foolish habits.

In other words, evil prospers where there is a spiritual vacuum. Each generation must evangelize its own population. We cannot rest upon the accomplishments of the past generation. Weeds of immorality soon thrive and grow fast. They take possession of a life, a nation, in a hurry. The penalty of neglect is decay and ruin. A Christian nation, a Christian family, a Christian life will deteriorate quickly if neglected.

GOODNESS REQUIRES CULTIVATION

Then I saw, and considered it well: I looked upon it, and received instruction.—Proverbs 24:32

You need do nothing to produce sin and ruin. Decay is a natural process because man is a sinner by nature. But if you wish to produce goodness, you must cultivate it. It is easier to keep a good farm good than it is to reclaim a farm that has deteriorated through neglect. And so it is with life.

Our nation was a spiritual nation at the turn of this century. But through false teaching, spiritual neglect, and a failure to evangelize the present generation, our nation has become a hotbed of hate, rebellion, and civil war. There was time when every city of our nation and every church held annual revival meetings. Colleges held two revival campaigns a year. It was difficult for a person to escape the net of evangelism. But today, there are few meetings, and seldom are there city-wide revival campaigns. The result is moral and spiritual decay.

Preachers formerly emphasized salvation, giving invitations for seekers of salvation to come forward in public confession of Christ. Seldom do we see this today!

We can save America, but it will require cultivation, weeding out sin, and seed sowing of the Word of God. We must water our garden with the tears of prayer, and hoe out the seeds of hate. The task of the church is stupendous. The challenge is great.

YOU CAN CHANGE THE WORLD

Yes, you can change the world! The world of the early church was wicked, immoral, pagan, and overrun with social

evils. One hundred and twenty converts tackled the job o.
preaching the gospel to a lost world. The Apostle Paul, on
man, evangelized the known world. Wherever the gospe
was preached, it brought light and deliverance.

Finney changed his world through revival.

Moody changed his world through revival.

Down through the centuries great men of God hav
changed their world.

You can change your world today!

Family Relationship

(Proverbs 1:8, 9; 3:1, 2; 4:1–4; 6:20–24; 7:1–3; 13:1;
15:5; 20:20)

*My son, forget not my law; but let thine heart keep my
commandments: For length of days, and long life, and
peace, shall they add to thee.*—Proverbs 3:1, 2

It is self-evident that God knew that children need parents,
else He would not have planned creation as He did. A baby
could not exist without parents. A growing child needs
guidance, care, and instruction. But just when do parents
lose their value? Birds raise their young and then cast them
from their nests, but they still teach them to forage for
themselves, to find food, and to avoid natural enemies.
Eventually, young birds leave their parents when they have
security and capability and no longer need their parents. But
just when do human children cease to need parental care?

Can we set a certain age? Or rather, shall we say that a
child needs parental care as long as he is not mature? He
needs guidance in meeting the temptations and issues of life.
He needs assistance until he is capable of self-support.

On the other hand, we should always honor our parents
and heed their experience, no matter how old we are. A
former governor of Alabama left his office and drove into
the country to his mother's cabin. He said, "Mother, I want
you to treat me like your boy again. I have become hard
and callous, until I have lost the human touch. I want my
soul restored."

His mother cooked his favorite meals, read the Bible to
him before he went to bed, and then had him kneel and
pray at her knee as he did when he was a little boy. Then
she tucked him into bed and kissed him as she did when he
was young.

The next morning, the governor kissed his mother goodbye, and drove back to the capitol to his office. Before leaving, he said, "Goodbye, Mom. You have restored my soul. I am human again. You have made me feel the love for humanity within my soul, which I had lost."

We will always need our parents!

But parents must remember it is their duty to teach their children. Too many are too busy to train their children.

Children profit by learning from their parents' experience. Why should they repeat their mistakes? It is wise to learn from their experience. It is foolish to ignore it.

Mere acceptance of parental authority is not enough. We must allow our parents' teaching of the Word of God to become a very part of our being. Our thoughts and our affections should be under the control of the spiritual laws of God which our parents have taught us. God pity the child who is without spiritual training and help from parents. Parents who fail to teach their children in the way of God have failed miserably.

Only fools ignore the training of spiritual parents. The wise will listen.

A WISE SON MAKETH HIS PARENTS GLAD

(Proverbs 10:1; 15:20; 22:6; 23:15)

A wise son maketh a glad father: but a foolish son is the heaviness of his mother.—Proverbs 10:1

Life's greatest treasure is a child who honors his parents. What a joy he brings! Parents rejoice at the time of birth and from that time they would lay down their very lives for their children. Parents are deservedly proud of children who make the honor roll in high school. They rejoice when marriage brings them into the fullness of life and the completion of maturity, and they establish a home.

One thing that makes a parent rejoice more than anything else is to have children who honor the Lord and who live a good life. Spiritual success is more important than business or financial success. For future happiness and successful living depend upon spiritual and moral principle.

A good life, free from trouble and heartache, is a Christian life. Children who drink and do evil bring great sorrow

A FOOLISH SON BRINGS SORROW

(Proverbs 17:25; 19:13, 26; 29:3)

A foolish son is a grief to his father, and bitterness to her that bare him.—Proverbs 17:25

Some years ago, a teen-ager was caught in the act of stealing a car. He fought a running gun battle with police in an effort to escape, but he was apprehended, arrested, and imprisoned. His parents were reputable people, and when they heard the news, their hair turned white overnight. Both died within six months after this incident.

A parent's heart beats for a son or daughter. If a child is in trouble, then the parents are in trouble. If the child suffers illness, the parents experience extreme anxiety. If the child sins, then the parents' hearts are broken. Parents are identified with their children, and this identity never ends.

A wayward child can put parents into an early grave. Grief is a cruel killer! A good child brings great joy. It is more humane to kill a parent with a knife than with sorrow!

For Peace of Mind

Do you desire peace of mind? Then you must avoid just eight things. Avoid these eight things as you would avoid a rattlesnake.

I. Be not envious

Be not thou envious against evil men, neither desire to be with them.—Proverbs 24:1

Too often we do envy the wicked when we see their wealth, possessions, and pleasure. Satan whispers in our ears, "If you would dip your colors and forget your high standards, you could own and drive the same car as the wicked man does. You could live in his mansion."

In Pslam 73, the Psalmist was also tempted, until he saw the ultimate end of the wicked man. The sinner may have pleasure, but he does not have peace and joy which the Christian has. In the end, he will be eternally lost!

II. Rejoice not over the defeat of thine enemy

Rejoice not when thine enemy falleth, and let not thine heart be glad when he stumbleth.—Proverbs 24:17

Some of our popular songs are built around the theme of personal satisfaction over the failure of the enemy. "I'll be glad when you cry," because "you made me cry," they sing. Note this is not a Christian's attitude! A Christian never wishes anyone evil or sorrow. Christ taught us to love our enemies, to do them good, and to seek to win them to Christ. Another person's sorrow, failure, or defeat will not improve your situation. Happiness over another person's sorrow reveals smallness, vindictiveness, and meanness within our own heart.

A mean spirit does not impart happiness, but rather

misery. A person who gloats over another's failure has a
sick soul. Let us pray for our enemies and make them our
friends.

III. Fret not

*Fret not thyself because of evil men, neither be thou
envious at the wicked.*—Proverbs 24:19

We live in the midst of trouble. The world is filled with
evil men, and the news is constantly bad. Recently a cartoon
appeared showing a stock broker, who said to his wife, "Isn't
it strange how the world has progressed the past century,
even though the news is always bad?"

Don't fret over evil-doers. Instead, go about doing good.
If the world were not evil, it wouldn't need you! Your light
shines the brighter because of the darkness which surrounds
you. Leave evil men with God. Be good yourself.

Philippians 4:1–9 gives us the secret of a happy life.
Think positively, not negatively. Think on good things, not
evil things. Fill your mind with things that bring joy, and
not with things which create worry and concern. There is so
much on earth that is good, why waste time dwelling upon
those things which bring defeat and fear?

IV. Meddle not

*My son, fear thou the Lord and the king: and meddle
not with them that are given to change.*—Proverbs
24:21

Some people, who are radicals, are given to change. Don't
meddle with them. Radicals always live short and turbulent
lives. If you cast your lot with them, you will go down in
defeat with them. Your life will be filled with trouble and
violence.

Instead of joining in with the radicals, walk discretely,
seeking to please the Lord and the authorities. Civil dis-
obedience is becoming very popular among those who yearn
for publicity, attention, and popularity. They are seeking
personal fame. Lawlessness attracts attention, without a
doubt, but it will not bring peace and happiness. Walk with
God and you will dwell in peace.

V. Respect not persons

These things also belong to the wise. It is not good to have respect of persons in judgment.—Proverbs 24:23

Treat all men kindly. Don't play favorites with the rich over the poor. Don't give preference to the popular person over the common person. All souls are precious to Christ. Don't enter into racial hatreds, or class hatreds. Love all men.

VI. Witness not without cause

Be not a witness against thy neighbour without cause; and deceive not with thy lips.—Proverbs 24:28

Don't be quick to condemn anyone. You will never regret what you do not say, but criticism can make an enemy out of a friend. Don't criticize. Swallow your words if they are a witness against another.

VII. Seek not vengeance

Say not, I will do so to him as he hath done to me: I will render to the man according to his work.—Proverbs 24:29

What satisfaction is there in "getting even" with another person? Let God be the judge, then you will not regret the person's calamity in his hour of reckoning. Let God vindicate you with His blessing, not with your enemy's failure.

VIII. Faint not

If thou faint in the day of adversity, thy strength is small.—Proverbs 24:10

When everything goes against you, don't faint. Instead, trust in the Lord and wait upon Him. If you give up and quit when things go wrong, you are very weak! Testings are blessings in disguise if you trust in the Lord.

New Testament Truths Based on Proverbs

TAKE THE LOWEST ROOM

Put not forth thyself in the presence of the king, and stand not in the place of great men: for better it is that it be said unto thee, Come up hither; than that thou shouldest be put lower in the presence of the prince whom thine eyes have not seen.—Proverbs 25:6, 7
Whosoever exalteth himself shall be abased; and he that humbleth himself shall be exalted.—Luke 14:11
—Read Luke 14:7–10 for complete passage.

So much of the New Testament is based on the book of Proverbs. This book is constantly quoted in Holy Scriptures. One could not possibly doubt its inspiration. Room does not permit us to reveal all of this similarity and all the quotations, in the New Testament from the book of Proverbs, but we will illustrate this fact with a few of these passages in the 25th chapter of Proverbs. This chapter seems to be of particular value in the New Testament.

Christ's parable in which he reveals the embarrassment of the man who exalts himself is found in embryo in Proverbs 25:6, 7.

Human nature is naturally proud, and seeks exaltation. Honor is due those who are faithful, but those who seek self-glorification are usually humiliated. No one appreciates a self-seeking person. Nothing brings disgrace quite as quickly as self-gratification.

Jesus had much to say on this subject. His own disciples sought human recognition and yearned for the prominent place in His future kingdom. And who will be the greatest in Christ's kingdom? Jesus Christ himself! Then He was the one most like a child! Did He not leave His eternal Kingdom to come in the flesh to die for us? (Philippians 2:3–11).

LOVE THINE ENEMY

(Proverbs 25:21–22; 24:29; Romans 12:17–21; Luke 6:27–36)

If thine enemy be hungry, give him bread to eat; and if he be thirsty, give him water to drink: for thou shalt heap coals of fire upon his head, and the Lord shall reward thee.—Proverbs 25:21–22

Love is the essence of Christianity. A true disciple of Christ is ruled by love, not by hate. He does not try to make evil right by returning vindictive acts for evil acts. Two wrongs never make one right. The Christian's weapon is love, and love will conquer when hate cannot.

A Mennonite in Pennsylvania, when awakened by a thief who stood over him with an axe, said, "My friend, the Lord would not let thee harm me. He would wither thine arm first!" Immediately strength left his assailant's arm. The Mennonite arose from his bed and awakened his wife, saying, "Wife! Wake up! This man is hungry. Otherwise he would not have broken into our house and attacked me. Get up and make him some dinner, so he can eat."

The thief was fed and sent away unharmed. His guilty conscience compelled him to give himself up to the law, but then the Mennonite refused to press charges against him.

PREACH THE GOSPEL

(Proverbs 25:25, 11–13; Matthew 4:17; 5:14–16; Mark 16:15)

A work fitly spoken is like apples of gold in pictures of silver.—Proverbs 25:11

The first and primary duty of the Christian is to witness to the lost, to bring them to Christ. Both the messenger and the message are important. The message is like cold water for a thirsty soul. The proverb says is like apples of gold in a silver frame. The sinner is hungry, lost, and under the condemnation of sin. The message of the gospel brings him hope and joy.

The messenger is also important. How beautiful are "the feet of him that bringeth good tidings, that publisheth peace." "How shall they believe without a preacher?" If we do not warn the wicked of the error of his way, he will die in his sins and be lost. The soul winner is so precious to the sinner, he is called the peacemaker, and men call him the child of God.

Christians are shining lights—the only light of the world. Christians are lights on candlesticks. They are to let their light so shine that men will see their good works, and glorify their Father in heaven.

EMPTY CLOUDS

Whoso boasteth himself of a false gift is like clouds and wind without rain.—Proverbs 25:14

Clouds they are without water, carried about of winds; trees whose fruit withereth, without fruit, twice dead, plucked up by the roots.—Jude 12

Ecclesiastes speaks of clouds also: "If the clouds be full of rain, they empty themselves upon the earth" (Ecclesiastes 11:3). The reason so many Christians never bless anyone is that they themselves are empty. Their own souls have not been charged with the blessing that comes from the infilling of the Holy Spirit. One cannot give out blessings from the Word of God to others until He himself has imbibed deeply of its truths.

In Jude 12, we read of those who are empty, who stand in the pulpit and do not give a blessing, because they themselves lack faith and have no faith to share with others. We must receive from above before we can give to those who live below.

Eight Well Known Adages

I. THE CONCEITED FOOL

As a dog returneth to his vomit, so a fool returneth to his folly. Seest thou a man wise in his own conceit? There is more hope of a fool than of him.—Proverbs 26:11, 12

There are many adages based on Scripture, particularly the book of Proverbs. It is amusing sometimes to hear people credit to the Bible proverbs that are not in the Bible. One lady had an entire neighborhood searching the Bible to find the saying, "Let every tub sit on its own bottom." Said her pastor, "Sister, though that adage is not in the Bible, nevertheless, you did a good thing when you asked your neighbors to search for it. At least you succeeded in getting them to read the Bible, and much good will accrue from it!"

When you do find a maxim in the Bible, it is of vital and living importance, for it teaches the way of life. The book of Proverbs is actually a book of Christian ethics, and its adages are most vital.

This adage, Proverbs 26:11, 12, is most common. How true it is that the sinners return to their sin even when it brings sickness upon them. They drink liquor, only to vomit it, but the return for more after the hangover is ended. They never learn from experience. Wine sores may cover their bodies and delirium tremens may drive them insane, but they will seek more wine!

Our proverb points out how foolish a person is to return to his sin. Why do men do this? Because they are slaves to Satan and their lusts. Christ alone makes them free. The world thinks Christians are crazy; but the sinner who returns to his sin is the foolish one.

II. DILIGENT IN BUSINESS

Seest thou a man diligent in his business? he shall stand before kings; he shall not stand before mean men.
—Proverbs 22:29

Poverty is no asset, nor is it a mark of spirituality. Not only does God's Word promise success to the industrious person, so does experience prove it. The person who works hard, is industrious, creative, and dependable is always rewarded. The person who is indolent is never successful. We should be good business men for God! Make all the money you can, so you can use it to preach the gospel.

III. THE FAITHFUL FRIEND

Faithful are the wounds of a friend, but the kisses of an enemy are deceitful.—Proverbs 27:6

The person who compliments you when you are wrong is not a friend but a flatterer. A true friend will love you in spite of your faults, but he will be faithful in telling you that you are wrong.
The friend of friends, that "sticketh closer than a brother," is Jesus Christ. He tells us we are sinners, but He offers forgiveness and salvation. He died for us when we were yet sinners.

IV. THE WANDERING BIRD

As a bird that wandereth from her nest, so is a man that wandereth from his place.—Proverbs 27:8

Many people never stick to anything, any task, or any location. Some ministers keep traveling from pulpit to pulpit, to escape trouble. But all places are the same, and all people are the same. It is better to be faithful, and to see your task through to the end, than to flee from trouble. Strong characters remain at their posts.

V. A GREEDY PERSON

Hell and destruction are never full; so the eyes of man are never satisfied.—Proverbs 27:20

The man who makes his first thousand thinks he will be satisfied, but he won't be. The more he makes, the more he wants. Satisfaction comes from resting in Christ.

Hell is never full! What a statement! Hell must be a b[...] place, and many people go there. There is always room f[...] one more, but make sure it isn't you.

VI. LACK OF VISION

Where there is no vision, the people perish: but he that keepeth the law, happy is he.—Proverbs 29:18

Vision is required to write music and literature. It tak[...] vision to invent machinery. Vision is required to build [...] business. But most important of all, vision is required if sou[...] are to be reached for Christ. Jesus told his disciples, "Li[...] up your eyes, and look on the fields; for they are whi[...] already to harvest" (John 4:35). Have you caught the visic[...] of lost souls? Millions are dying without Christ.

VII. REMOVE NOT THE ANCIENT LANDMARK

Remove not the ancient landmark, which thy fathers have set.—Proverbs 22:28

Rationalism and modernism is the curse of the churc[...] Don't try to improve on truth, salvation, and the Gospel. S[...] is old-fashioned, hell is old-fashioned, and only the ol[...] fashioned gospel can meet the need of man.

VIII. THE VINDICTIVE PERSON

Whoso diggeth a pit shall fall therein: and he that rolleth a stone, it will return upon him.—Proverbs 26:27

The prime example of this adage is Haman. (See Esth[...] 7:10.) He sought to hang Mordecai, and he himself hung o[...] the gallows which he had built for Mordecia. Don't buil[...] gallows for others; you will hang if you do!

Warning to Sinners

SIN'S PENALTY—GUILT

The wicked flee when no man pursueth: but the righteous are bold as a lion.—Proverbs 28:1

A few years ago, when I was chaplain at the Northeastern Federal Penitentiary, we visited an inmate who was about to be discharged after having served his sentence. He said, "I am glad I came to the penitentiary. A few years ago, I embezzled some money at the bank. Thereafter I could not sleep nights. Guilt hounded me night and day, and I lived in constant fear. When the bank examiners discovered my theft, I fled. After that I would flee from place to place, never staying in one place for very long. I constantly worried about the welfare of my wife and daughter. I would phone to inquire concerning them, and immediately I would flee, for I knew the FBI would dog my steps and follow up that call. It was a horrible life, and I lived in constant fear.

"One day, I went to the FBI office and surrendered. I was tried and sentenced. Now I have served my time, paid my debt, and I may return to my family to live with them in peace. I am glad the debt is paid, and I am forever free!"

The Christian is free from guilt and fear. Christ paid his debt on the cross. All guilt is forever gone. The life of the Christian is one of quiet and peace.

SELF-RIGHTEOUSNESS IS IMPOSSIBLE

He that covereth his sins shall not prosper; but whoso confesseth and forsaketh them shall have mercy.—Proverbs 28:13

It is natural for a man to deny sin and to seek to cover it. Men do this in self-defense. No one ever admits guilt if he can escape detection, unless, of course, he is seeking forgiveness from God. God will not forgive sin until it is

163

confessed and forgiveness sought. Christ didn't come to sa[ve] righteous men, but guilty men. All men are sinners.

As long as we cover our sins, guilt will devour our sou[l.] There will be no forgiveness nor deliverance from guilt. B[ut] as soon as we repent, forsake sin, and turn to Chr[ist] seeking forgiveness, that very moment we will find peace.

Man seeks to save himself through his own good works. [He] excuses his sins by comparing himself with other sinne[rs.] He tells himself he is no worse than anyone else, therefore [if] he is lost so will all men be lost. But he forgets that the[re] are a few of us who have confessed our guilt and soug[ht] and received forgiveness of sins.

Man cannot save himself. No matter how much good [he] does, he cannot undo a single sin. And even if he liv[ed] ever so righteously, his nature is sinful, and his very he[art] must be cleansed within.

So let us confess our sins and not cover them. Let [us] forsake them and prove our sincerity. And God promis[es] we will find mercy. Calvary extends mercy to us all.

SIN BRINGS SUDDEN DESTRUCTION

He that being often reproved hardeneth his neck, shall *suddenly be destroyed, and that without remedy.*—Proverbs 29:1 (Proverbs 12:28; 13:13).

An inebriated man awakened the minister in the middle [of] the night, calling from a saloon on the phone. He had ju[st] been shot in a drunken brawl. "Please come and pray f[or] me," he pled. "I've cursed you many times, but preacher, [if] I die, I know I'm a lost man. Please come and help me get right with God!"

The minister arose, dressed, and hurried down town to t[he] tavern and led the man to make a profession of faith [in] Christ. The new convert promised that he would come to t[he] church and be baptized as soon as he was well if G[od] would only spare his life. God did answer prayer, and [he] lived. But he did not come to church, not did he make [a] public confession, and he was not baptized.

A few weeks later, the minister saw him riding on [a] horse on a Sunday morning. He stopped him and remind[ed] him of his covenant with God. Once more he vowed [he] would come and make a public profession of faith. B[ut] he did not.

At the dinner table one night, the minister said, "There is going to be a very sudden death soon."

"Why do you say so?" his wife inquired.

"Because the Bible says, 'He that being often reproved hardeneth his neck, shall suddenly be destroyed, and that without remedy.' " He related how this man had made a covenant with God, had been spared as a result of prayer, and then had ignored constant warnings.

Two nights later, the phone rang, and that man's wife sobbed and said, "My husband has died very suddenly!"

God's Word warns us to come to Christ while we may (Isaiah 55:6). Now is the day of salvation (II Corinthians 6:2; Hebrews 3:7, 8).

Who Is God's Son?

*Who hath ascended up into heaven, or descended?
who hath gathered the wind in his fists? who hath
bound the waters in a garment? who hath established
all the ends of the earth? what is his name, and what is
his son's name, if thou canst tell?*—Proverbs 30:4

It is self-evident that the Creator is God. No man no
angel has the power of creation. Only God can bring matte
into existence. Genesis 1:1 says, "In the beginning, Go
created (made something out of nothing) the heaven(s
and the earth."

The word *God* is in the plural, including the entire Trinity
This plurality is repeated in Genesis 1:26: the plural nou
God is followed by a plural pronoun *us*. Often in the O
Testament Scriptures *God* is pural. For instance, i
Deuteronomy 6:4, "Hear, O Israel: the Lord our Go
(plural) is one (in the sense that there is none other) God.

In Psalm 110:1 the Father and the Son are mentione
together. In Isaiah 42:1 the Trinity is included in the on
verse. The Father speaks of placing the Holy Spirit on H
servent, His Son.

But in no place in the Old Testament is the Christ, the So
of God, described so definitely as in Proverbs 30:4. Her
Christ is described both as the Son of God and as th
Creator. Then the Son is the Creator, and He must there
fore be God! This same truth is taught in John 1:3, and i
Colossians 1:15–16.

A Jewish boy came to church one Sunday night an
avowed his purpose was to prove that Jesus Christ was n
God. When he was shown Proverbs 30:4 and asked, "O
whom is this speaking," he replied, "Of God, that is obvious

"Did you know then that God has a Son? And what is H
Son's name? Can you tell?"

He threw up his hands and said, "That does it! I cann

escape the truth of this Scripture. If I obeyed my own mind
and conscience, I would accept Christ as my Saviour, but
I don't dare!"

THE WORD

*Every word of God is pure: he is a shield unto them that
put their trust in him. Add thou not unto his words,
lest he reprove thee, and thou be found a liar.*—Proverbs 30:5, 6

John refers to Christ as the Word, or the Logos which
means the incarnate wisdom of God. Christ was a revelation of God. He was also a revelation of all truth, wisdom,
and knowledge. He knew the secrets of the universe, scientifically and historically. He knew the laws of the universe and
what held creation together, for all things consist in Him.
The Bible reveals Christ to us, but Christ also is the key
to the Bible. He is the living Word, producing the spiritual
truths of the Bible in daily life, in teachings, and in works.
He is the man of the book, and the Bible is the book of
the God-man. Proverbs 30:5, 6 foretells the coming revelation of the Son as a living Word. Here the Word is a person,
and we are to put our trust in Him. What a marvelous
revelation this is of the coming revelation of God through
both the Bible and through the Son. Could prophecy be
clearer? Surely Proverbs is a divine revelation also.

THE LORD

*Remove far from me vanity and lies . . . Lest I be full
and deny thee, and say, Who is the Lord? or lest I be
poor, and steal, and take the name of my God in vain.*
—Proverbs 30:8, 9

Proverbs connects the authority of Christ as the mainspring of our life and actions. Our words, our deeds are all
dependent upon our acknowledgement of the authority of
Christ as our Lord. Romans 10:9 states that we are saved
when we confess that Christ is our Lord (original rendering).
Too many people confess that they believe in Christ when
in truth they do not. For if we believe that Christ is God
and trust in Him for salvation, then we will also commit our
very life to His control and obey Him. We will make Christ
Lord as well as Saviour if we truly believe.

Could the case be stated any clearer than Proverbs state it? Verse 9 states that doubting God's Son as Lord will lead to sin and even cursing and taking the name of the Lord in vain. Is Christ precious to you? Do you obey His every command, and is your heart's desire to please Him? If He is Lord, then you do.

Lessons from Nature

There be three things which are too wonderful for me, yea, four which I know not: The way of an eagle in the air; the way of a serpent upon a rock; the way of a ship in the midst of the sea; and the way of a man with a maid.—Proverbs 30:18, 19

There are some things we see, which we know are so, even though we cannot understand them. Certain laws of nature are beyond human comprehension, but no one doubts them. Faith is a common commodity in life, and without it there would be no business transactions or progress in civilization. The skeptic says, "I will not believe unless I understand." But why apply this principle to religion and not in other walks of life? In the field of religion, above all others, faith is required, because man cannot expect to comprehend an infinite God with a finite mind. A God we could understand would be no God at all! If we must admit we cannot understand God, then we are only admitting that God is greater than we are. Some infidels ask questions which we are not able to answer, but all they prove is not that God does not exist, but that we are ignorant.

We cannot understand how a cow eats grass and makes milk with yellow butter, while a duck will eat the same grass and grow feathers, but we know it is so. The writer of Proverbs could not understand certain things in nature, but he knew they were so, so he believed them. No man has ever seen God at any time, the Son alone has revealed Him, but by faith we believe in Him. He has revealed Himself through nature, through divine revelation, and through the incarnation of His Son.

The infidel may deny God if he wishes, but I know He exists, for He dwells within my heart. I feel His presence; He has changed my life. We don't have to understand to believe,

nor must we be able to explain why things are so to make
them true. Faith is practical and common.

FOUR THINGS WHICH ARE SMALL BUT GREAT

*There be four things which are little upon the earth, but
they are exceeding wise: The ants are a people not
strong, but they prepare their meat in the summer; the
conies are but a feeble folk, yet make they their
houses in the rocks; the locusts have no king, yet go
they forth all of them by bands; the spider taketh hold
hold with her hands, and is in kings palaces.*—Proverbs
30:24-28

Most animals are created with some weapon of defense.
But some are not. Some are very small and insignificant.
But these small creatures exist, and some enjoy security
and even luxury, as does the spider who dwells in king's
palaces.

Smallness can become a source of security. The small is
unobserved and overlooked. Small creatures can go their own
way and not be bothered, whereas a larger animal might
be destroyed.

So there is a reward in not being great! Those who are
important face dangers the unimportant do not share. You
may consider that you are small and insignificant. If so
praise the Lord. God can use you as He could not use a great
person. He has chosen to use the small person, then the glory
of success will go to God and not to man.

The small man must use his brains to make up for the
lack of brawn. Steinmetz, broken in body and small in size,
could not play football as a boy, but he became one of the
greatest scientists in the field of electronics.

A blind man cannot see, but he develops senses which
the seeing person does not know exist. A blind man told
how he was fired from a railroad job because he could not
see. The result was that he had to learn to use his brain
instead of his muscles. He became professor of journalism at
Marshall University. Said he, "If I had not been almost blind
I would have been a miner instead of an educator." So you
see, smallness can become a great blessing.

FOUR COMELY THINGS

*There are three things which go well, yea, four are
comely in going: A lion which is strongest among beasts,*

*and turneth not away for any; a greyhound; an he goat
also; and a king, against whom there is no rising up.*
—Proverbs 30:29–31

Did you ever see a lion gracefully loping through the
grass? Or a he-goat leaping from one crag to another at a
dizzying height without slipping or falling? Or have you
beheld the majesty of a peacock which makes no apology
to anyone for his beauty? God made him that way! A king,
similarly, marches against foe without considering the danger
or consequences. None of these turn aside. They are masters
of the world! They do not know the meaning of the word
"can't," and they are not acquainted with the word "defeat." They walk into the face of death without quavering.

Christian, let this lesson be for you. If you are right and
just in your cause, never give up. Hold your head high. Stand
true. You will be comely as the animals who do not know
defeat!

The Perfect Wife

Who can find a virtuous woman? for her price is far above rubies.—Proverbs 31:10

Recently, in a restaurant, we saw a young mother drinkin beer, sucking a cigarette, and nursing her baby. The chil was dirty and needed attention, and her other children wer unruly, dirty, and poorly-clad. We pitied them.

We thought of our own mother, a godly Christian woman who sang her children to sleep to the tune of hymns. Sh taught us to pray at her knee and read Bible stories to u each night. She was a woman of great faith and she instille her faith into her children. What a contrast!

Every woman has a choice. She may be a woman whos price is far above the rubies, revered and loved by he husband, and adored by her children whom she has inspire to greatness. Or else she can be a woman who is a dis couragement to her husband, offering no hope to her chil dren. She may stoop to the lowest level.

No one can reach as low an ebb as a woman who doe not know God. On the other hand, no one inspires suc hope or challenges men to such aspirations as a good woman Christ makes the difference.

My mother said, "When you select a girl to be your wif choose the girl you wish to be the mother for your children.

A woman can make or break a man. She will eithe challenge him to greatness, or else she may ruin him foreve:

Abraham Lincoln's fiancée was asked, "What do you se in that homely man that would make you want to marr him?"

"I see the future president of the United States," sh answered.

"President? How could he ever be elected? He lacks th charm necessary for such a position."

"He will be president, for I shall make him presidential timber," she replied. And she did!

HER CHARACTER

The heart of her husband doth safely trust in her.— Proverbs 31:11 (Read Proverbs 31:11–28)

People don't change much over the years. A good wife and mother hasn't changed much from what she was four thousand years ago! It is true that her work is never done. Love is her motivating power, and she uses her ingenuity to care for her family.

Men are occupied in industry and put in definite hours, or else if they work in the field, they have general chores to do. Their work is planned. But a good mother never finishes her work. The business of running the house, buying and preparing the food, raising and caring for the children— these are among the multiplied duties of a mother. The occupation "housewife" is not to be looked down upon, for a good housewife must use her business ingenuity to make the money reach. Women always did hunt for bargains; they still do. Mother must care for both the children and her husband. She is responsible for the cleaning and furnishing of the home. She must be a specialist in economics, home economics, child care, child psychology, cooking, and a lover of the whole family.

A mother even upholsters, sews for the poor, promotes her husband socially, and she is also the backbone of the church. Of the two sexes, a woman must be the most versatile, industrious, and responsible. Don't underestimate her! She is a specialist in everything.

Don't call the woman the weaker sex. She creates life, cares for life from its birth, trains children, leads them in paths of righteousness, and endures hardships from her husband at times, who should, but doesn't, understand her problems, nor does he appreciate them. When the husband drinks and goes astray, she rises to the challenge and raises the children for God even under the pressures of persecution. If you have found a virtuous woman, you are most fortunate.

HER PRAISE

Her children rise up and call her blessed; her husband also, and he praiseth her.—Proverbs 31:28
(Read Proverbs 31:28–31)

Does a woman receive a reward for all of her efforts? When her children boast that mother is the best cook in the world, that is reward enough. Love, devotion, and adoration are rightfully hers, and children who have been raised by a godly mother will give her the devotion which is her due. There is no love on earth to compare with the love of a mother. There is no deeper love than that of a child who adores his mother. All wealth in the world could not purchase a mother's love. As a woman's children will say, "Mother, there are many women in the world, but you are the greatest of them all!" It is truly a privilege to be a Christian mother.

Listen to the story of christ

...from the moment of the Annunciation to the Ascension, dramatically recorded on ten long-playing stereo records. You'll feel the happiness and joy of Mary, running to tell of the angel Gabriel's visit. ■ You'll sense the worry of Mary and Joseph, searching the noisy crowds for their lost 12-year-old son. ■ You'll understand Peter's impulsiveness when you hear him splash into the water to swim ashore to his Master.

jesus: a Biography

The complete story on ten full stereophonic records in an attractive library case, with accompanying text. More than 200 writers, actors, musicians and technicians have added a new dimension to the living story of Jesus.

Ten inspiring records for only

$49.95

Available from your Christian bookstore or

Timothy Books
Newtown Industrial Commons
Newtown, PA 18940

Please send _____ sets of
JESUS: A BIOGRAPHY.

Name _____

Address _____

City _____

State _____ Zip _____

Enclose check or money order with coupon.

10 more
popular inspirational paperbacks from timothy books

1 Demons, the Bible and You—An anthology on the occult by Russell T. Hitt, J. Stafford Wright, William J. Peterson and other authorities on demonology and satanism.

2 Your God and Your Gold (Leslie B. Flynn)—A reminder to our materialistic culture of our stewardship responsibility.

3 Hell, You Say—Carl Johnson, well-known author and evangelist, analyzes the biblical view of hell

4 Health, Wealth and Happiness (Dr. Ralph W. Neighbour, Sr.)—Solomon's key to successful living, from the book of Proverbs.

5 Set Free (Addison C. Raws)—Seventeen men whose lives prove that no alcoholic needs to despair.

6 Go, Christian, Go—A primer on successful Christian living by William S. Deal.

7 It's About Time—Dr. Leslie Flynn discusses man's most valuable resource and how to make the most of it.

8 A Merry Heart—A storehouse of humor for speakers and masters of ceremonies, from toastmaster Dr. Russell Pavy.

9 On Our Way Rejoicing (Ingrid Trobisch)—The incredible saga of a great missionary family.

10 They Looked for a City (Lydia Buksbazen)—The gripping true story of a Jewish family and their bitter but triumphant struggle for survival.

Available from your Christian bookstore or

timothy books
Newtown Industrial Commons
Newtown, PA 18940